AN ENGLISH LADY IN CH

John Gross:—

ENTRANCE OF THE BRITISH CONSULATE-GENERAL AT KASHGAR.

An English Lady in Chinese Turkestan

Lady Macartney

With an Introduction by Peter Hopkirk

HONG KONG OXFORD
OXFORD UNIVERSITY PRESS
1985

Oxford University Press

Oxford New York Toronto
Petaling Jaya Singapore Hong Kong Tokyo
Delhi Bombay Calcutta Madras Karachi
Nairobi Dar es Salaam Cape Town
Melbourne Auckland

and associated companies in
Beirut Berlin Ibadan Nicosia

© Eric Macartney 1931
Introduction © Oxford University Press 1985

First published by Ernest Benn 1931
This edition reprinted, with permission
and with the addition of an Introduction,
in Oxford Paperbacks 1985

ISBN 0 19 583879 3

OXFORD is a trade mark of Oxford University Press

Printed in Hong Kong by Ko's Arts Printing Co.
Published by Oxford University Press, Warwick House, Hong Kong

INTRODUCTION

IN the heart of Central Asia, in China's great back-of-beyond, lies the remote frontier town of Kashgar (Kashi). Until very recently, when it was opened to foreign tourists, it was one of the least-visited places on earth. Not only is it politically sensitive, being close to the Russian frontier, but it has also always been a prisoner of its awesome surroundings.

To its east stretches the Taklamakan desert (Taklimaken Shamo), into whose treacherous sands entire caravans have been known to vanish without trace. On its other three sides it is cut off by high mountain ranges, the Tian Shan, the Pamir and, further south, the Karakoram. Over the centuries a sad procession of travellers have left their bones in the icy passes or in the burning desert. Before the coming of the telegraph and the aeroplane, the small mud-walled township of Kashgar was one of the loneliest and most inaccessible spots in the world.

But for more than fifty years it was Britain's most advanced position in the Great Game, that long and shadowy struggle with Tsarist Russia for political and economic supremacy in Asia. From the tiny Consulate-General, where fluttered the last Union Jack between India and the North Pole, a succession

of British Indian Government officials monitored and
reported back to their chiefs at home every Tsarist
(and later Bolshevik) move in the region. For at stake,
or so the strategists in London and Calcutta were convinced, was British India, the richest of all imperial
possessions.

Meanwhile, from their own Consulate-General
there, the Tsarists kept a like watch on British movements for their chiefs in St. Petersburg. For despite its
isolation, this otherwise insignificant oasis was ideally
situated for intelligence-gathering in what might be
termed the Victorian Cold War. Standing in neutral
territory, astride a busy caravan route, it lay midway
between the front lines of the two rival empires.

Sir George Macartney was the first Indian Government official to man the Kashgar listening-post. He
arrived there in 1890, at the age of 24, with Francis
Younghusband, just two years his senior. Little did he
dream that he was destined to spend the next twenty-
eight years, the whole of his career, in this desolate,
fly-blown town. Initially Macartney was appointed as
British Agent there, becoming Consul-General in
1912. He was knighted in 1913.

Officially, his role was to look after the interests
of the small British Indian community in Kashgar
and elsewhere in Chinese Turkestan, which consisted
entirely of native traders and money-lenders. But
unofficially he was there to keep a watch on Russian
machinations, and particularly those of the wily
Tsarist Consul, Nikolai Petrovsky, who had already
been in Kashgar for eight years when Macartney arrived, and had made himself its virtual ruler.

In this battle of wits, and of wills, the young
Macartney possessed one advantage which sprang
from his unusual family background. He was the son
of a Scottish father, Sir Halliday Macartney, and a
Chinese mother, of whom little is known (and to
whom he never referred, even to his children). As a
result, he spoke beautiful Chinese, was familiar with
the courtesies and the way of life of the Chinese
people, and became the recipient of their con-
fidences. He was thus able to establish a special rela-
tionship with the Taotai and other leading Chinese
officials which his abrasive Russian rival was denied.
Frightened of Petrovsky, it was to Macartney that they
came for advice, as well as to bring him the latest intelligence of what the formidable Russian Consul was
up to.

At times Macartney found Petrovsky perfectly af-
fable, but for the most part relations between the two
men were strained. Indeed, between November 1899
and June 1902, Petrovsky did not speak to his British
counterpart. This behaviour was especially bizarre in
so small a European community.

The trouble arose partly from Macartney's friendship with a Dutch priest, Father Hendricks, to whom
the Russian had taken a curious dislike. Not only did
Macartney enjoy the old priest's company, at a time
when he had no other friends in Kashgar, but he also
found him a most valuable source of intelligence. Sir
Aurel Stein, the Central Asian scholar and traveller,
called Hendricks 'a living newspaper'. Macartney and
Hendricks had only one language in common —
Latin. Macartney invited Hendricks to share his meals

and eventually to move into Chini Bagh (Chinese Garden), the house the local authorities had set aside for the British representative.

In 1898, when Macartney returned from leave in England with a bride (the author of this book), Hendricks insisted on moving out. Macartney managed to persuade the Chinese to find the Dutchman a house. However, for reasons which are not clear, Petrovsky put pressure on the Chinese to withdraw the offer. This resulted in popular demonstrations on behalf of the priest, whom the locals held in high esteem, and eventually he was found a rather squalid alternative home. Hendricks remained a close friend of the Macartneys until his death. Ironically he was given a splendid funeral by Petrovsky's successor, and was buried in the Russian (and only European) cemetery in Kashgar.

Macartney's bride was a girl with whom he had spent much of his childhood. Catherine Borland's parents were Scottish and came from Castle Douglas where her father, James Borland, had received his early education at the village school and had become a friend of Halliday Macartney. It was a friendship which was to last all their lives, and while Halliday Macartney was in China his eldest son George spent his holidays from Dulwich College with the Borland family. (James Borland was in shipping and the family lived for a time in Liverpool and then in London.) George and his future bride were thus more or less brought up together. After a two-year engagement, they were married in the autumn of 1898 following George's arrival, unexpected and unannounced, from

Kashgar. Catherine was just 21. She was to spend a total of seventeen years with her husband at Chini Bagh, where their hospitality became legendary among the few European travellers who passed through Kashgar. She was also to bear him two sons and a daughter, Eric, Robin, and Sylvia.

This delightful book, first published in 1931, describes day-to-day life in the remote and tiny community. It tells, too, of how Catherine gradually transformed the somewhat monastic establishment which her husband had shared with Father Hendricks into something resembling an English home. (She had even arranged for a small piano to be transported across Russia to Kashgar.) The book has its funny moments and its poignant ones. It also has its grim ones, like the scene they came upon as the whole family rode away from Kashgar through the mountains on their way home on leave in 1914:

Our horses saw it first and began to snort, and show signs of nervousness. Then we saw ahead of us and a little lower down, in a gloomy valley, a caravan of horses and men, the horses still standing but frozen to death, overcome probably by a blizzard. And there too were the vultures at their ghastly work, picking the skeletons clean. We slowly passed them in that veritable valley of death, and left the ghostly caravan behind us. But the memory of it remained with us for many days and nights...

There are some omissions, too. Lady Macartney relates how the discovery of an ancient and mysterious manuscript in the desert, followed by further acquisitions by her husband and Petrovsky, led to the eventual unearthing by Sir Aurel Stein and others of a previously unknown civilization on the ancient Silk Road. But she does not tell us about the race which

developed between the two men to buy such
manuscripts from native treasure-hunters after both
had been instructed by their governments to acquire
whatever they could.

Those obtained by Macartney, including many in
previously unknown scripts, eventually found their
way into the British Museum — but not for very long.
It was discovered that a native dealer named Islam
Akhun, who was principal supplier to both Macartney
and Petrovsky, had decided to take advantage of their
rivalry. His earlier finds were genuine enough, but he
was soon supplying both men with 'ancient'
manuscripts which he himself painstakingly manufac-
tured, thus saving himself long and dangerous
journeys into the Taklamakan.

Islam Akhun was eventually exposed by Sir Aurel
Stein who had become suspicious and who trapped
him into a full confession. If it was any comfort to
Macartney, Akhun's forgeries had not only deceived
Petrovsky, but had also made a fool of Dr Rudolf
Hoernle, an eminent British Asiatic scholar, who
wasted five years trying to decipher the illiterate
forger's invented 'scripts'.

Sir George Macartney served his country with ex-
ceptional devotion and brilliance, managing for many
years and virtually single-handed to hold back the
tide of Russian political influence in this crucial area.
Not only was he greatly loved by the Chinese and
their Muslim subjects, but he was also profoundly
respected by his Tsarist adversaries in this forerunner
to today's Cold War.

Unfortunately, being a man of great reticence, he

left no memoirs. Therefore this book, entrancing as it is in its own right, gains additional importance. However we are fortunate in having his official monthly Kashgar diaries and other intelligence reports, now in the India Office archives, and available to students of the Great Game era. It was largely from these, moreover, that one of his successors as Consul-General at Kashgar, Sir Clarmont Skrine, and Dr Pamela Nightingale, a modern historian, pieced together the story of his long years at Chini Bagh in their book, *Macartney at Kashgar*, published by Methuen in 1973, but now out of print and difficult to obtain.

After one final mission into Bolshevik Central Asia immediately after the Russian Revolution, Macartney retired from Indian Government service in 1919, settling with his wife on the Channel Island of Jersey. He was there throughout the German occupation of the island in the Second World War, dying on 19 May 1945 at the age of 78. Soon after the German surrender, Lady Macartney went to live with her son Eric and his wife at Charminster in Dorset, where she died in 1949.

She was thus spared the sadness of learning of the fate which befell her beloved Chini Bagh with the coming of the Chinese Revolution to Sinkiang (Xinjiang). While the former Russian Consulate-General is today used as an official guest-house, the Macartneys' former home came down in the world, becoming a shabby-looking hostel for long-distance truck drivers. Gone are the beautiful gardens on which Lady Macartney and her successors lavished years of care,

while the once grand Consulate building, now cracked and decaying, is merely a sad echo of its imperial
past.

Although she was the first mistress of Chini Bagh,
Lady Macartney was not alone in recording the high
days of this Great Game outpost. Two of her successors have left accounts of their days there, brief
though these were compared to Lady Macartney's
seventeen long but happy years. Ella Sykes, whose
brother stood in for Macartney when he and his family went home on leave in 1914, wrote *Through
Deserts and Oases of Central Asia*, to which her
brother contributed chapters on the history,
geography, and customs of the region. This was
published by Macmillan in 1920, and is now a rare
book. Diana Shipton, whose husband Eric Shipton
was British Consul-General at Kashgar after the Second World War, describes life there in *The Antique
Land*. This was published by Hodder and Stoughton
in 1950, and has now long been out of print.

There are four further accounts of life and work at
Chini Bagh. In 1926, Sir Clarmont Skrine published
Chinese Central Asia (Methuen). Nine years later
Colonel Percy Etherton wrote *In the Heart of Asia*
(Constable), which dealt with the first years following
the Bolsheviks' rise to power just across the frontier.
Finally, Eric Shipton wrote about his experiences in
Kashgar and the surrounding areas, although largely
from a mountaineer's viewpoint, in *Mountains of
Tartary* (Hodder and Stoughton, 1951), and in his
autobiography, *That Untravelled World*, also
published by Hodder and Stoughton, in 1969.

In addition, few travellers passing through Turkestan failed to record their impressions of this home-from-home in their books, or of the welcome, whatever their nationality, for which it was so celebrated. There may be little trace left of the Chini Bagh which Lady Macartney and her successors created, but it is certainly immortalized in the modern literature of Central Asia.

Peter Hopkirk is the author of three books on the Central Asian travellers: *Foreign Devils on the Silk Road*, *Trespassers on the Roof of the World*, and *Setting the East Ablaze*.

AN ENGLISH LADY IN CHINESE TURKESTAN

BY
LADY MACARTNEY

LONDON
Ernest Benn Limited

CONTENTS

CHAPTER

I. FROM LONDON TO KASHGAR . . . *page* 1

II. MY FIRST IMPRESSIONS OF CHINI-BAGH . ,, 32

III. MY EARLY DAYS IN KASHGAR . . . ,, 41

IV. AN OUTLOOK ON CHINESE TURKESTAN AS A
WHOLE . . . . . . ,, 51

V. THE MOHAMMEDAN, OR OLD CITY OF
KASHGAR . . . . . ,, 63

VI. THE CHINESE, OR NEW CITY, AND A CHINESE
DINNER . . . . . . ,, 76

VII. HOUSEKEEPING DIFFICULTIES . . . ,, 87

VIII. OUR FIRST LEAVE, AND RETURN TO KASHGAR
WITH AN INCREASED FAMILY . . ,, 103

IX. KASHGARI WOMEN . . . . ,, 121

X. A SUMMER HOLIDAY AMONG THE KIRGHIZ . ,, 136

XI. A JOURNEY HOME VIÂ NARYN AND CHIMKENT ,, 152

XII. THE CHINESE REVOLUTION . . . ,, 184

XIII. CHANGES IN KASHGAR . . . . ,, 201

XIV. GOOD-BYE TO KASHGAR, AND OUR JOURNEY
HOME THROUGH EUROPE IN WAR TIME ,, 217

INDEX . . . . ,, 233

LIST OF ILLUSTRATIONS

ENTRANCE OF THE BRITISH CONSULATE-GENERAL
AT KASHGAR . . . . . . *Frontispiece*

KASHGARI TRADERS WAITING TO RECEIVE US ON
THE ROADSIDE . . . . . . *Facing page* 30

A CHINESE TRAVELLING CART . . . . ,, 138

ON OUR WAY THROUGH THE THIAN-SHAN RANGE,
BETWEEN RUSSIAN AND CHINESE TURKESTAN ,, 220

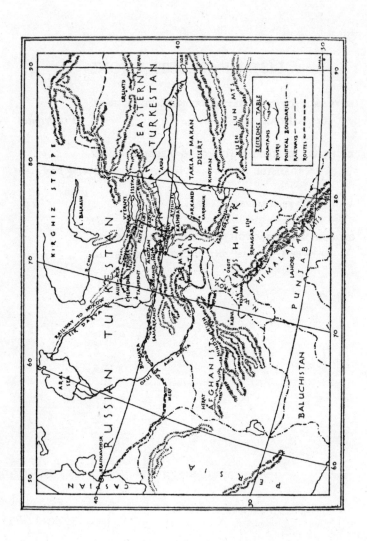

AN ENGLISH LADY IN CHINESE TURKESTAN

CHAPTER I

FROM LONDON TO KASHGAR

LONG years ago, one Saturday morning in early autumn, I, a girl of twenty-one, was busy in the kitchen making cakes. I had been engaged to be married for the past two years, and my fiancé, as I supposed, was away at his post in Kashgar. As my future life was to be spent in the wilds of Central Asia, I was doing my best to learn things that would be useful to me in such a remote place.

My thoughts were in far away Kashgar, while my hands were beating up eggs, for I was expecting to hear from my fiancé that he had got leave to come home to be married within the next few months.

Suddenly the front door bell rang loudly, and the maid went to answer it. Back she came running in great excitement with the astonishing announcement "Mr. Macartney has arrived." I simply did not believe her and told her not to be so silly, while I calmly finished my cake, and put it in the oven.

Then my mother called to me to come at once. Imagine my feelings when I saw my fiancé standing in the drawing-room; and when he calmly announced

that we must be married the next Saturday, and start
back to Kashgar as soon as possible afterwards, for he
had only got three months' leave from Kashgar, and
already five weeks of it had gone.

It seemed an utter impossibility to make all arrangements and get my things ready in a week, but all the
same we managed it, and were married on the 17th
September and left England and our friends on the
6th October 1898 to start out on our great adventure.

To me it was a great adventure indeed for I was
the most timid, unenterprising girl in the world. I
had hardly been beyond the limits of my own sheltered
home, and big family of brothers and sisters, had never
had any desire whatever to see the world, and certainly
had no qualifications for a pioneer's life, beyond being
able to make a cake.

Our honeymoon was spent in travelling across
Europe, through Russia, over the Caspian Sea, and
along the trans-Caspian railway to Andijan. Then
from Andijan to Osh by Russian tarantass, or post
cart, and from Osh to Kashgar, over the Thian-Shan
mountains on horseback. Quite a novelty in the way
of a honeymoon! To me, who had never travelled
before, it was all very strange and almost unreal, and
sometimes I had the feeling that I must be in a dream,
for my peaceful, uneventful life at home had been so
suddenly changed.

A journey of that sort is a pretty good test to one's
temper, for nerves get strained, at times almost to
breaking point. Everything seems to go wrong when
one is utterly tired out, and sometimes very hungry.

If two people can go through the test of such a journey without quarrelling seriously, they can get on under any circumstances. We just survived it, and it promised well for the long journey through life. But at times how desperately homesick I was! And especially so when we got into Russia, and I found I could speak to no one. What hurt me most was that I could not read a word in a newspaper, or even the name of a station or of a shop. And I had four long years of living in a strange land to look forward to before I saw home again.

When we were down near Rostov in South Russia my husband got out of the train one afternoon to get boiling water for our tea, and left me in the carriage to set out the cups and biscuits. It was the custom, when the train came to a station, to rush out armed with a kettle or teapot, race along the platform, to where there were several great *samovars* of boiling water presided over by peasant women, who charged 5 kopek or ¼d. for a kettleful, and back again before the train started. We had always found great fun in this bit of excitement until this fatal afternoon.

I was busy getting the tea things ready, when, suddenly to my horror the gong rang, and off the train started without my precious husband. For a few minutes I felt petrified by my tragedy. Here was I stranded in a country where I could not speak a word, with no money, no tickets, and, worst of all, no passport. After what seemed hours, but probably was not more than an hour, of acute agony of mind, wondering whether I should ever find my husband, or anyone I could speak to again in this lonely world, suddenly a raucous Cockney voice in the next carriage started singing a good old English music-hall ditty. How my heart rejoiced and my spirits rose. It was like an angel's song to me.

I rushed out into the corridor, and there met, emerging from his compartment, a big, florid-looking man, dressed in very large checked riding clothes, who was smoking a huge cigar while he sang gaily between the puffs "Knocked 'em in the Old Kent Road, ta-ra-ra." I told him my trouble, and he promised to help me through any difficulty about tickets or passport, and I felt I had a friend. While we were talking, who should appear but my lost husband, shivering, and blue with cold. He had jumped on the platform at the rear of the train when it started, and, finding the door into the corridor locked, had been obliged to stand out in the bitter wind until the guard came along, and let him in to find me absorbed in my new friend. We discovered later that he was a groom of the Tzar's Stables in St. Petersburg on his way to Rostov to buy horses. He was a most entertaining companion, full of funny stories, which he told in his quaint Cockney way.

But I made a vow never again to let my husband get out of the train without me, and always to have some money, and my passport on me.

We reached Petrovsk on the Caspian Sea just in time to see the boat for Krasnovodsk pulling out from the quay, and found to our vexation that we must wait three days for the next boat.

In Petrovsk I got my first taste of the East, for the people and the bazaars were more Turkish than Russian. There was little to do or see there, and we spent our time wandering along the shore by the intensely blue sea, the water of which they say is so buoyant that it is almost impossible to sink in it. The Caspian Sea is peculiar in that it lies below the level of the Mediterranean. It is very shallow and horribly choppy if there is any wind blowing.

Leaving Petrovsk we sailed down the coast to pick up passengers at Baku.

Baku was rather a wonderful sight at night with the sky red and lurid from the reflection of the burning oil wells. Oil was everywhere, the sea was thick with it, the air heavy with the smell of it, and some years later, when we went by train from Baku, we saw it oozing out of the ground, and dripping down the railway cuttings. The boats and trains were all run by naphtha.

Krasnovodsk, on the Asiatic side of the Caspian, was reached next morning after a rather uncomfortable night.

We found that food was included in the price of the boat ticket, and thought what a good plan that was, but we altered our minds when we discovered that no meals were served until the boat was well out to sea, and no one wanted any dinner.

Krasnovodsk from the sea looked just a collection of bare white rocks and hills, white houses, with a few dusty miserable-looking trees. There is no fresh water there at all and practically no rain, and every drop of water used has to be distilled from the sea and it has a nasty flat taste.

But I.was greatly impressed by seeing a tall Russian fisherman walk up the pier with a huge sturgeon on his back. The head of the fish was a foot above his head, while its tail trailed on the ground. By this time we had become much addicted to·sturgeon, and fresh caviare, which were always served well cooked and in different forms at the railway restaurants.

We left Krasnovodsk in a very slow-going naphtha-driven train, and at once got into dry desert country through which we trundled peacefully, at times having to stop and wait while stray cows and calves belonging to the railway workers strolled leisurely off the line. Once the engine stopped and began hissing out steam furiously. When we looked out to see what was the matter, there was an old gander with his flock of geese calmly waddling across the line, regardless of the train, which must wait their pleasure.

Now, except for a cottage or two near the stations, all was desert country, across which great caravans of camels, each led by a little donkey, often riderless, but attached to the camels following, were continually trailing towards the Persian Mountains that could be seen on the horizon to the south.

At last, after two days of most monotonous scenery, which however turned wonderfully fascinating with the gorgeous colouring of the sunsets, away in the distance we saw a streak of water and knew that we must be getting near the ancient city of Bukhara, and that this must be the Oxus River, or, as it is now called, the Amu Daria.

On coming nearer, we saw a rickety wooden bridge ahead of us, and wondered whether we were expected to trust ourselves and the train to it. Evidently we were, for the train stopped, and the guard got out. Then we started on to the bridge at a slow crawl, with the guard walking ahead waving a red flag, and looking to see how much more had fallen away since the last train crossed. What the red flag could do to help us, I have never quite understood, for we did not need to be told that there was danger.

Slowly we went on with the whole structure swaying, and creaking, as though it was strained to its utmost limit of endurance. In places great beams had gone and we looked down the holes to the chocolate-coloured river rushing beneath us.

It took us over half an hour to reach solid ground on the other side, and until we felt we could breathe freely again. Still, in spite of its unsafe appearance, the bridge was used for some time after we crossed it, without accident. Four years later, when we travelled home, we found that a fine iron bridge had been built for the railway, though the old wooden one, or some of it at least, was standing to remind us of an anxious half hour.

Bukhara, much as we would have liked to visit it, had to be passed, and seen only from the station, but we greatly admired the fine-looking men and women we saw on the platform.

And so we came to Samarkand, where we were obliged to break our journey.

At that time, 1898, the railway beyond Samarkand to Andijan was only just completed, and was not yet open to regular passenger traffic, and a permit to travel on it had to be obtained from the Governor of Samarkand.

There were no proper carriages running, passengers having to go in covered cattle trucks. We saw some of these filled with *mujiks*, who squatted or lay on the floor, which was covered with straw. The prospect of being herded with them for several days was not alluring, but we could not see how it was possible to do otherwise.

Next morning we went to see General Medinsky, the Governor. We had no introduction to him, and we wondered how he would receive us, knowing nothing whatever about us. But we got the kindliest reception from him. We found him a smart and refined gentleman, every inch a soldier, and a man who inspired respect and confidence immediately. As he spoke only Russian, and my husband spoke French better than Russian, General Medinsky called his secretary to interpret. To our surprise, we found that she was an Irish girl, who had lived in Russia all her life, and who spoke Russian and French perfectly, but little English.

We were given the permit at once, and General Medinsky offered that, as his daughter was travelling in two or three days to Margillan to join her husband, who was stationed on the Pamirs, we should have a

coupé in a first class carriage he was having specially
run for his daughter. Of course we were delighted
with our good fortune.

As we had a few days to wait for our travelling companion, we set about to see as much as possible of the
City which had been the Cradle of the Mogul dynasty
that had ruled India for so long. We explored the
bazaars, saw the tomb of the Emperor Tamerlane,
covered with probably the largest slab of jade that has
ever been found, and the old gateways faced with
beautiful blue tiles that shone and glittered in the clear
dry air. But everything was crumbling, and these
ancient buildings were rather typical of the Tartar race,
whose splendour too had decayed. Now the Russians are the soldiers and conquerors, and the Tartars
the tradespeople and servants.

What struck me very much was the type of people
we met in Russian Turkestan. Many of them were
fair skinned, and European-looking. The men were
tall and dignified, and the women mostly were very
beautiful, with straight, regular features, and they
carried themselves with grace and elegance ; people
who, in spite of the Turkish and Mongol invasions,
had retained their Iranian characteristics.

Then there were others who, through intermarriage
in former times with the invaders, have developed the
almond eyes and high cheek bones of the Tartars and
Mongols.

General Medinsky was at the station to see us all off,
and we found quite a luxurious compartment on the
train reserved for us, for which we were duly thankful.

We found later that General Medinsky was well known to the Chinese in connection with the delimitation of the Russo-Chinese frontier between Kashgaria and Ferghana, for which he had been Russian Commissioner.

And so we started off in great comfort. However, we got rather a shock as we came near Margillan and found that, as our travelling companion was leaving the train, the first class carriage was being taken off, and we had to find accommodation in a crowded cattle truck.

My heart as usual failed me, for I had not yet learnt the art of not crossing bridges till I came to them— an art every good traveller must learn. We had another twenty-four hours to Andijan, and it looked as though we were in for a pretty uncomfortable time, for the train was crowded. But our luck was in again. A Russian officer we had spoken to several times was also leaving the train, and he offered us his wagon to finish the journey in. He had it all to himself, and had furnished it with a carpet of sorts, a table and chairs, and a native string bed with pillows, and rugs. Of course we accepted it most gratefully, and I began to realize how utterly useless it is to worry about difficulties lying ahead.

Our officer friend told us, too, that there was an Englishman on the train somewhere, herded with the crowd in one of the wagons, who was very uncomfortable. So we set about to find him. Everyone on the platform was wearing Russian fur caps and great coats and we were not very hopeful of recog-

nizing an Englishman. As all the headgear was much
the same, we began studying the footwear, but there
seemed to be nothing except long Russian boots, and
we were about to return to the train when, suddenly, an
unmistakable pair of English laced boots came marching
along. My husband accosted the owner with " Hallo,
you are the Englishman, aren't you ? " " Yes, I am,"
he said, " but how did you know ? " " By your
boots," we chanted in duet. We shook hands effusively,
as though we had been friends all our lives. He told
us he was John Speke, from London, and we introduced ourselves. Years after we met again at the
Royal Geographical Society, in London, and instinc-
tively looked at each other's footgear.

So having found a comfortable corner for ourselves, we felt that the least we could do was to share
it, and Mr. Speke gladly transferred his belongings to
our " Pullman."

I have never done such a funny journey before or
since as that one from Samarkand to Andijan. The
train meandered along at about fifteen miles an hour,
stopping whenever the engine felt so inclined. Passengers got out and picked flowers, and wandered
about the fields till the engine shrieked, and a gong,
made from a bit of railway line, sounded, when we all
scrambled back into our respective wagons. This was
rather a gymnastic feat, for they were so high from the
ground, and had no steps of any sort.

On the train was a shop, where things of every sort
could be bought,—meat, groceries, stores, brooms,
pots, pans, sweets, materials, paraffin, vodka, etc., and

at the stations, people were waiting to do their shopping and, of course, the train must wait till everyone was supplied, and had finished gossiping. So it is not surprising that the train was about a day late in arriving in Andijan.

Some fierce looking Caucasians, in their tight-fitting, full-skirted black coats, decorated with many cartridge pockets across the breast, high boots, huge fur hats rather like Busbys, and belts bristling with weapons, elected to call on us that evening. As the train did not stop to let them return to their own wagons when they felt sleepy, they just stretched themselves out on the floor, and went to sleep. I lay down on the one and only bed, and my husband and Mr. Speke arranged themselves on the floor each side of me, and we slept, my last thought being " What would my mother say if she could see me now ! " And so we slept peacefully until the train stopped with a bump, and we found that we were in Andijan, the terminus of the Central Asian Railway, on which we had travelled its whole length. It was now the end of October, frosty, and bitterly cold, and I can feel now the chilliness, and misery of waking suddenly in that icy cold wagon and having to turn out into the gloom of a half-lit station at five in the morning.

Some rather disreputable-looking Andijanis shouldered our baggage, and we walked up the village street, by the light of the stars, to a shabby hotel, where we had to put up for a day, and a night. The good lady of the house, who always had her head bundled up in a shawl, was quite friendly, and anxious to please us, but her ways and ideas were not ours, and after seeing her turn the soup we had left in our plates back into the tureen for the next comers, we were not so keen on the meals she put before us. Probably if we had not seen her methods, we should have thought her cooking quite good.

But it was such a relief to be able to have a change of clothes, for we had not undressed for many days.

Our two servants from Kashgar should have met us at the station, but they were nowhere to be found, and we were rather worried as to how we were to make up our caravan, and get across the mountains. The brilliant idea came to us to go to the station when the next train arrived, and sure enough we found them. They had missed us the night before in the dark. We greeted each other joyfully, for they too were feeling like lost sheep.

These two men had been with my husband for many years, and were very proud at being chosen to escort the new Memsahib.

I felt at once that they and I would be real friends, and I think the liking was mutual, for they were always my most faithful servants, and devoted helpers.

By coming to the end of the railway lines, we felt that we were leaving European civilization behind altogether, and now our real adventures into the unknown, for me at least, would begin by the fresh experience of doing a whole day's journey by Russian tarantass from Andijan to Osh, at the foot of the mountains we were to cross.

It was not altogether a painless experience, for the

tarantass has no springs. It is a boat-shaped basket resting on long poles, and drawn by three horses abreast. The central horse runs in the shafts with a big hoop over his head, which holds the shafts apart. He trots all the time, while the two outside horses, which draw from the axle of the front wheels, go at a gallop with their heads turned outwards. A big bell hangs from the hoop, and smaller ones are attached to the harness of all the horses, and they make a merry jingle.

We packed ourselves into the tarantass, sitting on rugs, and pillows, and when we were comfortably settled, the *yamstchik* or driver mounted the box. He was a very picturesque figure in his coat padded so thickly that it made him look enormously stout. It was fitted to the waist and very full in the skirt, and he wore a fur cap drawn well over his ears. He gathered up the reins and wound them round and round his hands to give him a good grip. This rather worried me, for I wondered why he needed to have such a firm hold, and I soon found out.

All this time the three horses were being held by a man, who had his work cut out to keep them still. When everything was ready, the *yamstchik* cracked his whip and the man holding the horses jumped cleverly aside. Up reared the horses, and away we bounded full speed, with all the bells jingling, dust rising in clouds, and people, dogs, and cats, chickens, and ducks scuttling out of the way for dear life. A very effective start, and one that necessitated a firm hold on the reins.

We reached Osh in the evening after breaking our journey halfway to change horses, and to have our lunch which at Russian post stations consisted of hard boiled eggs, bread, sometimes butter, and always tea, and a *samovar* of boiling water with which to make the tea. The *samovar* is a big urn made of copper, brass, or silver, in which water is boiled by charcoal being burnt in a tube or cylinder running through the centre of the urn, and it plays a great part in a Russian household, being the hot water supply for making tea, and coffee, boiling eggs, etc., heating water for the baby's bath, and for general household purposes.

A dozen eggs at least were brought for the two of us, and if we had been Russians, we should have eaten them and maybe have called for more.

The Russian tea I had come to like, especially when we were able to have slices of lemon in it, which the Russians take instead of milk. If lemons are not handy they even put a spoonful of jam or fruit juice in a glass of tea. Russian tea is always served in glasses and not cups.

The bread was mostly good, though they had one kind that was almost black and quite sour which I could not get used to.

But the dust on the road was suffocating, and we reached Osh covered with it, and shaken to pieces. Some hours later, our servants arrived in native carts with the baggage. These Andijani carts are very quaint. Made all of wood, they have wheels at least six feet high, and the driver sits on the horse's back with his feet on the shafts. Passengers, and luggage are put into a great basket-like cage. Of course they go at not more than a walking pace, or a very gentle trot.

Osh is a very pretty little Russian town, with a big native bazaar, situated at the foot of the Thian-Shan Mountains. Thian-Shan means Celestial, though the Chinese sometimes call them the Onion Mountains because of the wild onions that grow everywhere.

The Russians lay out their towns very prettily, with broad avenues of trees, mostly acacias, and in Osh clear streams run everywhere, bringing down icy cold water from the mountains. Rustic bridges carry the roads over the streams, and make it all delightfully picturesque ; and one begins to feel there the bracing air of the mountains.

We found that Colonel Zaitseff, the *Ouyiezd* Nachalnik, or district officer of Osh, had made arrangements for us to stay at the Club, where we found comfortable rooms prepared for our use, which, after the railway carriage we had lived in so long, seemed quite palatial. A Cossack, too, was deputed to wait on us.

A few days' rest in comfort was very welcome, while our caravan was got together.

Mme. Zaitseff invited us to dinner at their beautiful house perched up on the hillside above the town, and there we were received with the greatest hospitality and friendliness, for my husband had made their acquaintance when he was on his way home to fetch me. In spite of the language difficulty, I could not but enjoy our visit. He had evidently told them that I sang a bit, for they insisted on my singing. The only instrument they had was a nice little harmonium, and the only thing I felt I could sing to a harmonium accompaniment on a Sunday afternoon was a hymn. So I sang a good old Church hymn in English and could not help feeling that I was " singing the songs of Zion in a strange land."

They offered to sell us the instrument, as they did not use it, and we bought it to take along with us as a companion to a little portable piano we had bought in England and which was being sent direct to Kashgar. This tiny piano was made by Cramer. It had five octaves, and stood on a table. The keyboard could be lifted out and packed in a separate case by itself, thus making a horse load, with the case containing the keyboard on one side, and the case containing the action on the other.

When we left Osh Mme. Zaitseff sent us a goodly supply of bread and cakes for the journey, for which we were very grateful. We had to carry food for the sixteen days along with us, and knew that only live sheep would be available on the road, and certainly no bread.

At last the ponies were brought to the Club and loaded with our belongings, which included tents (in case of need), bedding, cooking pots and pans, food, and store boxes, harmonium, and grain for the horses.

When they came to load the harmonium, it was found to be too heavy for a horse to take over the steep roads that lay before us, and a yâk had to be found. This conclusion was arrived at only after much shouting and gesticulating. My husband said " Bund-o-bast karo," and very soon a yâk arrived with two Kirghiz, one driving and the other dragging the great shaggy beast, which seemed to be all head and body, and no legs. I had already discovered what magic those words worked. " Bund-o-bast-karo " means " Make arrangements," and arrangements are made forthwith, with no trouble to oneself, and all is peaceful once more. It is often not advisable to enquire too closely how arrangements are made, for frequently the result is acquired in a very high-handed way. Anyhow a good old grunting yâk appeared forthwith, the harmonium was hoisted up and fastened on his back and away he strolled leisurely with it. A yâk never hurries under any circumstance, and grunts and grumbles all the time.

Off we started, making an imposing procession, the yâk leading, followed by eight or nine baggage horses, while we and the servants brought up the rear on horseback.

I had never ridden before, and had no idea what I must suffer to become a horsewoman. My pony was saddled with a native saddle that had a high peak in front; it was well padded with a folded blanket, and another blanket was rolled up and strapped behind to make a support and give some warmth. I was to ride astride for safety on the bad roads.

The first difficulty was to mount. Every time I tried, I got my leg stuck on the rolled blanket behind, and I had to be rescued from my perilous position. At last, to help me, Jafar Ali, our servant, gave me a great heave up behind. Over went my leg and I nearly shot clean over the horse ; and becoming weak with laughing did not help matters.

Finally I was mounted, and off we started, I innocently thinking how comfortable it was to travel on horseback. After the first hour I began to feel stiff, then I got stiffer, until I was simply in agony, and felt as though every joint in my body was dislocated. Each movement and jolt was excruciating, but I dare not stop and dismount, for I was sure that in my present condition I should never be able to swing my leg over that bundle again.

So on we went for six hours, and when at last we got to the Russian rest house where we were to put up for the night, I had to be almost carried in, and laid down gently on some bedding, feeling the most miserably homesick creature in existence. How was I to live through sixteen awful days of such travelling ? I was quite sure I should not survive it, and I must confess that I pulled the blanket over my head and wept bitterly.

Next morning I could hardly rise, and getting dressed was too painful for words. But there was nothing else to be done but mount that horrible pony again, and exist through another day's torture. I finished that march not quite such a complete wreck as I had anticipated, and, to my surprise, in a few days I found myself actually enjoying the splendid scenery we were passing through, and forgetting that I was on horseback.

We wended our way through beautiful valleys, always ascending. Sometimes we were in a narrow gorge, with high rocks on either side, following a path beside a stream that leapt over great boulders, splashing us as we went along. Then across a little rustic bridge to the other side of the stream; and so backwards and forwards for many miles, until we suddenly left the gorge, and turned into a wide grassy valley of rolling meadows through which a broad, shallow river flowed peacefully along.

At this time of the year the water was low, and the rivers quite easy to splash through; but when I did the same journey four years later, it was in June, when the rivers were in flood, and they were a very different proposition then. The places where it was at all possible to ford were a quarter of a mile wide, and then so deep that we must cross on camels, while the ponies had to swim.

A camel is safe so long as he is in his depth, but if he once gets out of it, he has no idea of swimming, and just turns over and lets himself be washed away. Only once in all my journeys did I ford a river when it was considered unsafe to ride a camel. That time I was put on a great Chinese horse, like an old omnibus horse, behind a Chinaman who was used to fording that bit of the river. Seeing I looked frightened, my good old servant Jafar Ali patted my knee in a fatherly way, and told me to shut my eyes tight and keep them shut; I did, and did not open them till I knew that we were safely on dry land again. But it was horrible to feel the horse going out of his depth, and being carried along by the stream.

The first time I mounted a camel I was scared to

death. I was to get up behind a Kirghiz, who was
seated on the squatting camel. Every time I tried to
mount, the beast swung round his head with a snarl
to bite my leg, and I ran away. At last I managed to
get on when he was not looking ; my guide held my
hands round his waist, and shouted at the camel. Up
he got, hind legs first, pitching me forward on top of
the Kirghiz, and then with a violent heave up came
his front feet and I was bumped upright again. Away
we started at a trot across the sand, and I bounced
about in all directions, till we came to the water, and
slowly went down into it deeper and deeper ; branches
of trees and débris swirled round us and we seemed to
be making no headway whatever, but were just drifting
down the stream. In my terror I clutched frantically
at my guide, till I heard my husband calling to me not
to hug him so tightly. We got to the middle of the
stream, and I thought the end had come when my
companion began to say his prayers. I had been saying
mine all the time, but I thought it must really be serious
for him to do so. I shut my eyes, and tried to think
of other things—of anything I thought but of that
water whirling round us, making me feel as though I
must fall into it—and waited for the end. Presently I
heard a shout, and opening my eyes found that, instead
of drowning, we had reached the other side, but that
the river had washed away the bank and there was a
deep cutting about four feet high. A man was standing there, and my guide threw him the camel's rope ;
they both let out a stupendous yell, and my man
whacked the camel while he got tight hold of my

hands in front of him. Up shot the camel with a great leap, and for a moment we were nearly vertical; I should most certainly have gone off backwards if the Kirghiz had not had hold of my hands. The poor beast landed on his knees, and broke down the bank, and in a few moments I found myself sitting by the roadside wondering whether to laugh, or cry. Even my husband, the coolest and calmest of men, got rather a shock watching the camel's antics from behind.

Happily I was spared such thrilling experiences on my first mountain journey.

After five days' marching, we came to the foot of the big pass, the Terek Dowan, 13,000 feet. This pass crosses the very ridge of the Thian-Shan Mountains. We passed the night in a little rest house perched up on the mountain side, in which we found an iron stove and a plentiful supply of wood, kept there for travellers. As we were at an altitude then of about 10,000 feet, we needed the warmth, for the cold was intense. All night it snowed heavily, and we began to fear that we might be delayed; but next morning we found that the storm was over, and the sun was beginning to turn the mountains pink. By the time we were ready to start, it was shining brightly, and all promised well for our crossing of the pass.

As all signs of the road were obliterated by the snow, the Kirghiz with the yâks suggested that, as they knew every inch of the pass, they should go first, and we could follow in their tracks. We had had to arrange for yâks to take the most of the baggage over the pass, as they are more surefooted than horses, and accustomed to the rarefied air.

We were all suffering from mountain sickness, and it was a great effort to do anything, even to move ; the violent headache, and shortness of breath were very unpleasant and distressing, and we had had little sleep. But at last we were all mounted, and away we started to climb up and up the long narrow valley, our pace getting slower and slower, and the halts more frequent. Both the Kirghiz and the ponies relieved their feelings of discomfort by eating the snow.

The stillness and the silence grew more and more impressive. No one seemed to want to speak ; the song of the birds we had heard lower down had ceased ; and the thud of the horses' feet was muffled by the deep snow. The only sound to be heard was the laboured breathing of the horses, who could take very few steps at a time. We seemed to have left the old earth far below, and to have come into a new world—a world of silence, and whiteness, of brilliant sunshine, and dazzling blue sky.

We all wore dark goggles, and protected our faces as much as possible, but all the same we got very blistered and burnt. The caravan men pulled hairs out of the ponies' tails, and made a fringe of them under their caps to protect their eyes and faces. One stupid man took no precautions, and the result was that he went quite blind with the glare, and had to be led about for some days until happily he recovered his sight.

At last, with a final effort, we gained the summit, and found that it was almost as sharp as a knife. A pony could hardly get all four feet on the actual point. But what a vision opened out before us ! As far as eye could see there were snow mountains ; the sun making their peaks glitter, and sparkle, and turning their glaciers into mirrors ; while down their sloping sides it cast patches of wonderful blue shadow. Never had I imagined anything so magnificent and awe in-spiring, as I stood there spellbound ; all the fatigue and petty discomforts we had suffered were nothing to pay for this privilege of being on the mountain top. I felt so elated, and wanted someone to share my rapture. My husband was not near, so I turned to one of our servants and said with my very few words of Hindu-stani : " Look, how beautiful ! " He looked so puzzled and asked, searching on the ground at his feet : " What is beautiful ? " " All this," I said, waving my arm around. But he could not see what I meant at all. To him, it was just a difficult part of the journey that gave him a headache, and he wanted to get down to his lunch of bread and tea. So, disappointed, I had to keep my rapture to myself, and pass on to make room for others coming up.

The first part of the descent was very steep and rocky, and we preferred to walk, or rather slide, until the road was easier for riding.

A great change had come over the scenery, for we had crossed the very crest of the Thian Shan range. As the wind charged with moisture generally blows from the south west, it is intercepted by the mountains. So now we were in their rain shadow, and that fact made a tremendous difference, for the rain was stopped by the mountain range. On the Russian side, there is plenty of rain and snow, and consequently rich vegetation, while on the Chinese side, where we were now, the country was as dry as Egypt, and there was nothing but barren rocks to be seen. The only places that would be green now would be the valleys that were watered by springs and streams fed by the melting snow and glaciers of the high mountains.

These streams we followed all the way down to Kashgar. Trickling down the hillsides from the very top of the mountains into the valleys, they joined others and made larger streams which, in their turn, joined up with streams from side valleys, until at last they became a wide river, the Kizil Su, or Red River, which ran on through Kashgar, then through Maralbashi and finally emptied itself into Lop Nor Lake. I was greatly interested when my husband explained to me that we were now seeing the "Waterworks" of Chinese Turkestan.

At one place a clear stream we were following was joined by a stream of red muddy water, coming from a side valley. These two ran together side by side, with one half of the stream red and the other clear. The clear stream had come over white hard rocks, while the other had come down over soft red earth. I am afraid the muddy water got the upper hand, for the river, when it reached Kashgar, was well named the Kizil-Su, or Red River, it being just the colour of chocolate, and as thick.

Our second march, after crossing the Terek Pass, brought us to the Russian Frontier Post, Irkeshtam.

There we found a white Fort perched up on a hill, in which was an officer and a "*sotnia*" (100) of Cossacks.

Down by the river was a collection of whitewashed houses and sheds, and these we found to be the Customs Offices.

Mons. Tzagan, the Customs Officer, rode out to meet us, and invited us to stay with him, which we were very glad to do. We found a cosy room prepared for us, and a good meal on the table. How thoroughly we appreciated the comfort of being in a home for a few hours ; and of having a well-cooked dinner, without the flavour of smoke in everything. In the evening the Cossack Officer came in and we had a merry time, though I felt rather out of things not understanding Russian, and became very sleepy with the warmth of the room.

Mons. Tzagan regaled us with thrilling stories of his experiences in hunting and trapping smugglers. His work was to inspect caravans coming into Russia from Chinese Turkestan. The chief things smuggled were coral, Indian muslin for turbans, and *nasha* or *hashish*, the hemp smoked by the natives. Coral and muslin were highly dutiable, and *nasha* was prohibited. The caravan men had many tricks for hiding *nasha* and muslin, such as winding the muslin round and round their bodies and hiding the *nasha* in the folds, etc. But their mode of getting coral across the frontier was quite original. The ponies were made to swallow the beads and lumps of coral before reaching Irkeshtam. After the Customs inspection was over, the men were in a great hurry to get on, for they must watch the ponies' droppings carefully to regain their smuggled coral. So it was Mons. Tzagan's policy to detain suspected caravans as long as possible.

Irkeshtam must have been a very bleak and desolate place to live in, and I think the Russians were only too glad to see some fresh European faces; even if they were only British ones.

When we were going to bed that night, our host told us not to be alarmed if we heard some shots fired, for every night he had to go out and fire some rounds outside the compound to scare away the wolves, which would come right into his courtyard and attack the horses, or carry off any sheep or fowls they could find.

Next morning our Russian friends gave us a supply of fresh bread to carry on with us, and rode out some distance to see us off.

Our second march from Irkeshtam brought us to the Chinese Fort at Ullughchat. Not wishing to put up at the Fort in the midst of a lot of Chinese soldiers, who would be unpleasantly curious, we were passing some distance away across the plain when we saw the Chinese Commander coming to meet us. He was so pressing that, at least, we should go and have some tea with him, that we were obliged.to turn and go with him to his house, stared at, all the time, by a crowd of disreputable-looking soldiers. But we insisted that we must push on further that day to a big Kirghiz encampment, where we had made arrangements to stay.

The Kirghiz are a nomad people living in the mountains in big round felt-covered tents, or *akois*. But more about them later !

We found the encampment in a wide grassy valley, beside a river of crystal-clear water ; the grass was high and rich, and in it were growing masses of blue iris and tall yellow king cups. Tents were dotted all over the valley, and camels, yâks, horses, sheep, and goats were grazing everywhere. In the afternoon light, it was such a beautiful pastoral scene, and I wondered whether Abraham and his people had not lived in just such a place.

The head of the family or tribe greeted us with great friendliness, and showed us to the best and largest tent, putting tea, and bread of a sort, and little sour cheeses before us. The people were very curious to see us, and crowded round the door of the tent to get a glimpse of the strange English woman. We could not very well turn them away, as we were their guests ; but after I had received some of the chief ladies, and their children, our servants tactfully suggested that the *memsahib* must be tired and would want to rest. So we were left in peace.

But all the time baby animals kept nosing their way in. The Kirghiz bring up the baby animals in the tents with them, and they so felt they had the right to come in. I went outside for a stroll after dark, and got such a fright when a big shaggy head, with a very wet nose, was suddenly poked under my arm with a grunt, and I found I was embracing a little yâk, who had either mistaken me for his mother, or felt lonely and wanted sympathy.

We watched a very charming scene at sunset when the mother animals came running home to be milked. The women took them all in turn, starting with the goats and sheep, and each one chose out its own baby to lick and fondle while it was being milked. Next came the yâk cows and mares, which stood perfectly quiet until they were released to feed their own offspring and go off for a frolic together in the meadow. Then we heard a great commotion : the little camels began to cry and whine with excitement, and away in the distance we heard their cries being answered by their mothers, which were charging home at full speed. The mothers and babies greeted each other with delight, and then took their turn to be milked. It was very funny to see the women having to stand up for the operation with the milking pail on the stool. They brought us a bowl of camel's milk, and it was really delicious, just like thick cream.

I went away next morning with the feeling that the life of the Kirghiz was not so bad.

At last the day came when we crossed the final pass and found ourselves at our last camp, Mingyol, with nothing but a great stony desert between us and Kashgar, twenty miles away ; and on the sixteenth day from Osh we set out on our last march.

Very soon after starting we were met by a number of Cossacks, with a comfortable little carriage, very kindly sent out for us by Mons. Petrovsky, the Russian Consul at Kashgar, to bring us triumphantly home ; and my husband and I gladly dismounted, and got into the carriage, the Cossacks closed round us, and our caravan brought up the rear.

At places all the way along the route we found people waiting for us with refreshments spread out, of which we partook—Chinese, Kashgaris, Indians, Hindus, Russians, Afghans, and a Swedish Missionary, Mr. Högberg, who to my great joy I found spoke English fluently.

Each time we started afresh more people joined the procession, until there were some hundreds of horsemen trotting beside and behind us; we were enveloped in clouds of dust, and the excitement was great. Once a little calf in a field caught the infection and joined in the mad career, capering along beside our carriage for some miles : I have often wondered whether he was ever found again by his owner.

When at last we arrived at Chini Bagh (Chinese Garden), my new home, we found decorations up, the courtyard carpeted with bright rugs, and hung round with beautiful Benares brocade, to welcome us. A number of Hindus, dressed in spotless white, were drawn up as a guard of honour in two lines, and as we walked between them they bowed and salaamed, calling us "Ma Bap," which means "Father and Mother." I was very puzzled by their offering me rupees in the palm of their hands, and started to make a collection, when I saw my husband frowning at me and signalling to me that I was only to touch the money and pass on. Afterwards he explained that they were honouring me by paying me tribute and were not offering me tips !

KASHGARI TRADERS WAITING TO RECEIVE US ON THE ROADSIDE.

It was a very kind welcome, but I did wish I had been able to tidy myself up first. I was conscious all the time of looking like a dust heap, and could feel my hair walking down my back. Knowing that one is thoroughly untidy and dirty does not make one feel at all dignified.

In the drawing-room Mrs. Högberg was waiting for us with a very hearty welcome, and a real English tea prepared. And so we had reached home after six weeks' journey from London.

CHAPTER II

MY FIRST IMPRESSIONS OF CHINI-BAGH

NEXT morning I tasted one of the great joys of having done such a journey—the joy of waking up in a comfortable bed to the realization that there was no hurry to get up and start off again.

We had mostly slept on the hard, and often lumpy ground that even our mattresses would not soften, and I had become quite expert in curling myself round the protruding bits of rock sticking out of the earth. The fatigue and strong air however had made us sleep soundly in spite of discomfort; but I was very joyfully surprised to find here a bed ready for me, with a box spring mattress. It had been made by a Russian officer for his wife, and my husband had bought it from him at a great price when they left Kashgar.

To my English idea, the house was very quaint. It was built all on one floor on account to the frequent earthquakes, on three sides of a courtyard. The fourth side comprised the entrance gate, and servants' waiting rooms, where someone was always on duty to demand the business of anybody wanting to enter.

When I looked out of my window, I was surprised to find that we were rather alarmingly near the edge of a high cliff, the window being only six feet from it.

This exalted position gave us a beautiful view, reaching away to the snow mountains we had crossed.

Below us ran a road along which a continuous stream of loaded and ridden donkeys and horses seemed to be passing. Beyond the road were what had been in summer, fields of melon, rice, cotton, and clover, but now were dried-up stubble, in ground that was white and covered with saltpetre. This white powdery stuff comes through to the surface of the ground, as soon as it has ceased to be worked. I have heard that it is good for melons, and for that reason the melons of Kashgar are some of the finest in the world.

In the midst of the fields was a sad little triangular bit of ground enclosed by a mud wall, and in it were a few mounds of earth, and Russian crosses. It was the Russian Cemetery. Beyond it I could see the Kashgar river—the Kizil-Su—where a lot of horses were being watered by boys riding naked on their bare backs, into the deep water. How they ever kept their seats on a horse's wet bare back in that birthday costume was a wonder to me: only a rope was round the horse's head and yet they had perfect control. Then there were crowds of donkeys having their pails filled by men and boys with water to be sold in the city.

Away on the other side of the river, the dyers were at work laying out their long strips of cotton cloth they had dyed a lovely shade of deep red with dye made from the black hollyhock flowers.

Across the bridge lower down the river, one long stream of people, carts, and animals passed all day long. Everyone seemed to be singing or shouting, and now and again a queer long drawn-out note sounded through the general hubbub. The millers at the many mills along the river were calling, by blowing through rams' horns, for more flour to grind.

Behind the river, with its life and sound, were loess cliffs, terraced fields and trees, and beyond them the desert and white mountains of the Thian-Shan.

We went up on the flat roof of the house, and there away to the West and South were the snow giants of the Pamirs, with Kongur peak, which is nearly 24,000 feet, the tallest of them all, standing like a huge white wall, and looking in the clear morning air so much nearer than they really were. It was rare to get a clear view of them, for the dust haze, that was mostly in the air, made the visibility very bad, especially in the spring and summer, when, for weeks together, the air was not really clear, though the sun was able to shine through the haze.

The house had originally been a native dwelling, built round a courtyard, and like all native houses had no windows, the rooms being lit by skylights. Eastern houses always look so forbidding and uninteresting, for all that can be seen from the outside is a high mud wall.

The walls were about two feet thick and were of sun-baked brick, covered outside with mud, and inside they were plastered with gypsum to make them smooth and white. I soon found the comfort of thick walls, for they kept the house warm in winter, and cool in summer.

When my husband first went to Kashgar in 1890, he and Captain Younghusband, as he then was, were taken to this same native house and garden, which twenty-four years later became the British Consulate General. The old building was razed to the ground, and an imposing European house erected on the same site.

When I arrived in 1898 the Europeanizing had already begun. Glass was almost unknown in Kashgar, and oiled paper was used for the windows ; and they were an improvement on the skylights. Mons. Petrovsky had, as a great mark of friendship, lent my husband a large pane of glass in a frame for one window, but unfortunately before long they had a quarrel, and the precious piece of glass had to be returned.

Large iron Russian stoves had taken the place of the huge native fireplaces that gave little warmth, but plenty of smoke ; and the floors had been levelled. In a native room about three-quarters of the floor space is raised about two feet, making a platform which is covered thickly with carpets for people to sit and sleep on. But the funny little doorways with double doors, that one must stoop to go through, and the many niches in the walls, remained. I loved the fancy shaped niches, and they were certainly very useful.

One great day, soon after my arrival, a Russian merchant came with a caravan of window glass, which we Europeans bought up eagerly ; it was very bad glass, and everything seen through it was distorted. I often amused myself by watching people through it, laughing at the weird figures• they presented as they walked along. But it was glass, and it let in the sunlight.

Later we put up a verandah, which improved the look of the house vastly. It was rather unfortunate that the native workmen forgot to fasten the parts together firmly, so that it fell down like a card house with the first sharp earthquake. It was put up again, but more securely this time.

Our furniture was very primitive. Of course, it was all home made, and of white unpainted wood, as there was neither paint nor varnish to be got. The chairs were most original, and amused me mightily.

When my husband found himself stranded in Kashgar, his only friend was a Dutch Roman Catholic priest called Father Hendricks. I will give his history later. These two decided that they must make some chairs, as they had only the floor, or boxes to sit on. They neither of them were cabinet makers, and had no idea of designing a comfortable chair. The first one to be evolved showed strong monastic influence from Father Hendricks' early days. It was so high that I had almost to climb up to the seat, and must sit with my feet on the rail, or with them dangling. The back was quite straight and reached far above my head, and the seat was not more than about six inches wide. There was no possible chance of having a rest in it— all one's time was taken up with keeping oneself balanced. Then there were chairs of the same style, each a little less like a choir stall in an ancient chapel. At last one was made that had some degree of comfort, but was terribly hard, the seat not being shaped at all.

When Mr. Högberg came, he tried making a rocking chair, which my husband bought from him. For some unknown reason, when you sat in it, your head and feet rocked while your body remained still, and you felt thoroughly foolish. So the rockers were cut off, and at last we had a comfortable rest chair, for the back and seat were of stretched carpet, which was soft and restful.

But bright carpets, table cloths, and cushions covered a lot of faults, and when I had made a green silk shade for our paraffin lamp, the place looked very cosy and homelike. Very soon we managed to get some Austrian bentwood chairs and an American rocker that rocked properly.

One of my first ordeals was to make a tour of inspection, and have my staff properly introduced to me. We went first to see the cook in the kitchen, and I got my first shock. We entered through a very small door and found ourselves in a dark smoky room, lit only by a skylight. Sitting on the mud floor was our Indian cook with a Kashgar boy beside him helping him to make a cake. He had a basin of eggs before him, and was breaking each into his dirty brown hand, letting the whites slide through his fingers into one basin, and putting the yolks into another. I suppose he saw the look of disgust on my face, for he remarked that it would be better if I went away, and judged him by the excellence of his meals and not by his kitchen. He certainly sent us in wonderfully good things, but sometimes I wished I had not seen him at work.

We had five private servants, *i.e.*, cook, kitchen

man, house-table man, groom, and gardener. The gardener was a tiny little old man, a Kashgari, almost a dwarf, who always spoke as though his plants held conversations with him. If you asked him whether the peas would be up soon, he quaintly answered : " They tell me they will be coming out to-morrow." Then there were three Government servants, the Jemadar and two Chuprassis, who wore startling red and gold uniforms and huge white turbans, and rode before my husband when he paid official visits. And lastly four men to carry our post to the next Indian Post Office, ten or fifteen days' journey from Kashgar, according to the weather and time of year.

I felt awfully shy, and scared of this noble army, for I could not speak to them, and the only way I could show my kindly feeling was by smiling and nodding. One so soon feels foolish and self-conscious doing nothing but that. But they were all so kind and willing to help me, that I very soon felt quite at home with them and would have trusted myself with them anywhere.

To complete the British Colony, there were two Indian Munshis (or Secretaries) and a Chinese Munshi, all with their families, also an Indian Hospital Assistant as our medical adviser. They, and the servants had their homes just outside our compound, and we made quite a village of our own.

We had a large picturesque garden, laid out on two levels, with a flight of steps leading from one to the other. The upper garden was the orchard, and kitchen garden, and it was full of the most wonderful peaches, apricots, figs, pomegranates, and black and white mulberries; and later my husband grafted on to the native stocks English apples, pears, plums, green-gages, cherries, etc., from cuttings sent out from home. I think there is hardly a place in the world for fruit-growing like Kashgar.

The lower garden was shady with willows, elms, poplars, and a native tree called Jigda.

Against, and sheltered by the house, was a large vinery which my husband assured me would bear loads of grapes. Now all I could see was a wooden trellis and a mound of earth. Grapes, figs and pomegranates are all buried in winter to protect them from the frost.

The most fascinating part of the whole garden was the terrace that ran the entire length of it; it was walled in by a fancy wall of an open-work pattern, while tall straight poplars bordered the path. From this terrace one could look over the whole country and watch the life on the road and fields, and away in the river bed.

In the centre of the garden was the pond that, in spring, would store the water for garden use. Now it, and all the little irrigation canals that ran in all directions, were dry. Not a leaf was left on a tree, nor was there a blade of grass to be seen. It would have been too desolate for words in winter if the sun had not done his best to brighten things up, while the dust storms were quiet.

I was more than glad to find that my husband had a family of dogs, for I could talk to them and they took me to their hearts at once. My husband, during his years of loneliness, had gone in for many strange pets, some of which I could not help being very thankful had not survived. Wolves, leopards, and foxes did not appeal to me. The stags and gazelles I loved, and soon after my arrival I had a pair of tame geese given to me, which insisted on coming into the house to live, and while the goose was busy sitting on her eggs, Mr. Gander sat close up to me in the drawing-room for company in his loneliness.

A few weeks after my arrival, Mrs. Raquette, one of the Swedish ladies, gave me the sweetest little kitten, who at once asserted himself by flying at the dogs and turning them out of the room. He grew into an enormous cat, and was afterwards called by our children " Uncle Pussy," until he died of a good old age seventeen years later, only a very short time before we left Kashgar for good.

CHAPTER III

MY EARLY DAYS IN KASHGAR

OF course, people began calling on me at once, and I think everyone was anxious to see what sort of a wife my husband had found.

The Chinese Ambans came, but the only one I received was Yang-Ta-jen, the Hsie-tai, or Colonel of the troops in the old Kashgar City.

I was greatly interested in watching the arrival of my first Chinese visitor. He was escorted by a swarm of followers in the weirdest costumes and uniforms, and a crowd of boys who had joined his procession as it came through the bazaars. His sedan chair was lowered outside the gate of the courtyard, where my husband, who had had warning that he was arriving, went to meet him. After elaborate bows and curtseys to each other when, to my mind, they both looked as though they were trying to pick up something from the ground with the right hand by only bending the knees, they started towards the house, holding hands, and swinging them as they walked. This custom of holding hands seems to be reserved by the Chinese as a special mark of friendship for a foreigner, for they do not do it among themselves. Some of our English visitors found it to be rather embarrassing. But my husband entered into the

spirit of all the strange customs with the utmost
solemnity, often to my great amusement : he even
made the Kow-tow, when the solemnity of the
occasion demanded it. This performance he reserved
chiefly for funerals. One of the chief Ambans, the
Tao-Tai, died. He had been a great friend of my
husband's and, of course, the latter wanted to show
every respect to his memory. On the day when the
huge, red coffin, surmounted by an enormous paper
stork, was to be put in the Chinese graveyard, to await
the last journey back to China, my husband joined the
cortège at the Mission Station. He was in full
uniform, very tight fitting but smart-looking. The
cortège stopped when he was seen waiting, and
the chief mourner, dressed in white, knelt down
beside the coffin and kow-towed to my husband.
The least he could do was to return it. So down
he went in all the dust of the road and made his
kow-tow before the gaze of a huge crowd of people.
It was a difficult performance, for his uniform was so
tight that he could hardly bend ; his sword had to be
kept out of the way and his hat held on. He got
up covered with dust and took his place in the procession. I, with the Högbergs, was watching it all
with the keenest interest and amusement and a little
anxiety also as to whether his clothes would stand the
strain.

But I must go back to the arrival of the Hsie-tai.
My husband and his guest were preceded by Jafar Ali,
our Jemadar, arrayed in his red and gold uniform,
surmounted by a spotless turban, carrying aloft before

him the big red visiting-card of the visitor. At the drawing-room door he solemnly announced the name and rank.

One day I was watching these proceedings, and a funny thing happened. My husband and the visitor stopped for some reason on the way. Jafar Ali, not knowing that they were not behind him, walked up to the drawing-room door and impressively made his announcement. The look of surprise on his face was too funny for words when he discovered that he was alone. Back he went to look for the two lost ones, and this time he was careful to keep one eye looking round the corner to make sure that they did not play him that trick again.

Yang-Ta-jen was a very charming old man, polished and courteous in manner, and an old friend of my husband's. As my husband had been received by his wife, he returned the compliment to him. To the others I was " not at home," or as the Chinese say to excuse themselves, " The honour is too great."

The Hsie-tai asked if he might bring his wife and daughter to see me, and I fixed a day for them to come, though I could not imagine how I would entertain them. They arrived in grand style in sedan chairs, and carts drawn by fine mules, and I found that I had many more visitors than I had expected, for besides Yang-Ta-jen and his wife and daughter, a number of lady relations and their children had accepted my invitation. And of course they had brought swarms of servants, who tried to crowd into the room to see and hear all that was going on. The Chinese never seemed to mind having a lot of people around listening to everything that was said.

It was quite an undertaking to get the ladies with their tiny bound feet safely into the house. They walked with great difficulty, and must be supported by their attendants.

I felt terribly shy and awkward, not knowing what was the right thing to do, and, of course, I could speak to no one.

After we had given them tea, I took them all over the house, opened the cupboards and drawers in the bedroom and let them see all my clothes, which entertained and delighted them very much.

The daughter, a girl of about fifteen, looked very ill and seemed to be in pain. My husband asked her father what was the matter with her and he replied that she was ill because her feet were bound too late, after the bones were firm. He had been told by an English doctor that she would go into consumption if they did not unbind her feet and let her run about out of doors. But what would be the good of that, he asked, for no one would marry her with big feet and so she might as well be dead. It was not want of love at all, but he was worried to know which of the two evils to choose. Happily now that custom is almost a thing of the past in China, but in those days if one argued about it with the Chinese, they asked if their custom was any worse than ours of tight lacing, and that was a difficult question to answer.

My next visitor was an Indian lady, the wife of one of the Munshis. As she was a purdah lady, who was always veiled outside her own home and was never seen by men who were not of her immediate family, my husband and the men servants had to be banished before she would enter the house, and even then she kept her tent-like veil over her until she was safely in the room, and the door was shut. She brought me as a present some beautiful embroidery she had worked herself, and she sat, and talked and ate sweets till I became thoroughly bored. Then she began to yawn, but still she stayed, and I racked my brains to think of a way to get rid of her. The strain of entertaining someone I could not understand or speak to for nearly two hours was making me feel hysterical. At last our dinner gong sounded and I stood up. Up she jumped, looking so relieved, and hurried away. Then my husband told me that I, as hostess, should have given her the sign to go. If the gong had not sounded, we might have sat there all the evening, both feeling desperate, and yet afraid to make the first move. I wondered if I ever should learn how to do the right thing in such a topsy-turvy country.

Then the Chinese Munshi brought his wife to see me. When they came into the room, I was writing a letter home. They looked at my letter and my pen and then asked my husband whether I was really writing, or only pretending to. When they heard that I could both read and write, they were wonderfully impressed, and agreed that I was a great scholar for a woman.

My little piano which had just arrived interested them, and when I played it they were delighted to see the hammers dancing on the strings. My husband told me to sing something, and I sang a song in my very best style, feeling very pleased with the impression I was evidently making. They never took their eyes off me, and sat and listened as though they were simply enraptured : but to my utter astonishment when I had finished, they just collapsed in peals of laughter. I did not know what to make of this merriment. Were they amused at my comical performance, or was this the Chinese way of showing appreciation ? Anyhow, the only thing to do to save the situation was to laugh too, and we all roared with laughter together. But it was rather a shock to my vanity. Since hearing Chinese music I have come to the conclusion that mine must have seemed as funny to them as theirs does to us.

When one of the Indian Munshis came and asked me to " decompose " on the piano, I thought that the less I paraded my musical abilities the better !

My poor little piano had had a bad time on the journey. It was packed in zinc-lined cases, which were soldered down. At the Russian frontier these had been opened, and the zinc linings cut by curious Customs officials, who had never troubled to have them soldered up again, or the cases even screwed down securely. The result was that while fording the rivers in the mountains, water got into the packing cases, and there remained swishing about inside the piano for days.

When, eventually the piano arrived in Kashgar, and we unpacked it, we found that the keys were so swollen that they would not move, and the metal parts and strings were thick with rust. Mr. Högberg came to our aid, and took the whole thing to pieces. When the wooden parts were dried and the strings cleaned, with careful adjustment the piano was got into working order, and was little the worse for its adventures, which I think speaks very highly for Cramer's excellent little instrument.

It was a great joy to me to find there were two Swedish ladies at the Mission Station who spoke English, and the day after our arrival we went to see them. They were living just outside the city wall in an adapted native house, and their colony consisted of Mr. and Mrs. Högberg, and their little girl and boy, aged about nine and four, respectively, and Dr. and Mrs. Raquette. They all welcomed me with the utmost friendliness, and I felt at once that we would be lasting friends, and indeed we were that during all the years we were in Kashgar together. I do not know what I should have done without their sympathy and ever-ready help. The Högberg children soon became attached to me, and I taught Elsa English, and found her a splendid companion when she came and spent long days with me.

They were having very uphill work among the natives, and at times the feeling was hostile against them. But they worked on patiently, chiefly doing medical work, and teaching the children. Mr. Högberg was a very clever worker and could do and make anything he put his hand to. He did splendid work in teaching the native workmen to make furniture, build houses, make tools, and implements, etc., and so he gained their respect and confidence.

Dr. Raquette spent a great deal of time working on translations of the Bible, hymns, tracts, etc., into Turki, and now, probably, he is recognized in Europe as the foremost Turki scholar.

Then I must call at the Russian Consulate on Mme. Kolokoloff, the wife of the Secretary of the Consulate. Mons. Petrovsky had not his wife with him. There were two other Russian ladies, wives of the Cossack and Customs Officers, but as they spoke only Russian, I could not get on very well with them, and the visits we paid each other were rather painful ordeals. Mme. Kolokoloff spoke French, and so I set to at once to improve my French, and we got on splendidly with her and her three children.

There remains one more European to mention, Father Hendricks, the Dutch priest. He had been a great companion to my husband during the ten years he had been in Kashgar, and they had lived together. He was a highly intellectual man, who spoke many languages and who took the keenest interest in politics and everything that went on in the world. We nicknamed him the "Newspaper," for he ran about all day visiting, collecting and distributing news. He had been a missionary sent out by some society, but had been turned out for disobeying rules and orders. Then he was given a little Church in Holland, which he soon deserted and, running away to the East, settled himself in Kashgar.

He was a quaint figure, dressed in a dirty Chinese

coat and dilapidated black clerical hat, and always ran along as though he were in a great hurry to get somewhere and do something very important. He lived quite alone in a dirty hovel in the City, where he made quantities of wine each autumn for the Mass he read every day by himself. His altar was a packing case covered with a dirty lace cloth : soap and water did not come into his scheme of life at all. He spoke of his converts, but we never came across any, and we came to the conclusion that on that one subject he was a bit touched. But, in spite of his eccentricities, he was a very lovable character, always bright and jolly. He had no income whatever, and lived on gifts and meals he got from his friends. My husband has often said that the first ten years of his life, exiled in such a place as Kashgar, when he was little more than a boy, would have been unbearable without the companionship of Father Hendricks.

I started right away reading French with him, and was soon able, after a fashion, to converse with the Russians. It was a great sorrow to us when my husband, one day, found the poor old man lying dead all alone in his miserable hovel. We had known for some time that he was dying of cancer in the throat, and had offered to take him in and nurse him. But his one desire seemed to be alone, and alone he died. Only the day before, he had been to see us, looking terribly ill and very feeble, but, in spite of the agony he was enduring, he had a smile and a cheery word for our baby girl, to whom he was much attached.

So our society was rather mixed—cosmopolitan, I

might say, and very bewildering for a girl who had never left a very quiet sheltered home before.

Soon after my arrival, Christmas came round and we were invited to the Russian Consulate to celebrate their Christmas, thirteen days after ours. We all danced round the Tree and sang Christmas hymns to well-known tunes, each in our own language. And at the supper table eight different languages were being spoken—Russian, English, Swedish, French, Chinese, Turki, Hindustani, and Persian.

CHAPTER IV

AN OUTLOOK ON CHINESE TURKESTAN
AS A WHOLE

As I write my book, now and again the feeling comes over me that I am confining myself too much to my home and immediate surroundings, and that, all the while my readers—those of them at any rate who like to take a wide view of things—will be wondering if I have not something to say on Chinese Turkestan as a whole, and, incidentally, on our interests in that part of the world.

For such readers I am going to prepare in this chapter a miscellany of facts—some geographical, some archæological, and others political.

Now what exactly do we mean by Chinese, or Eastern Turkestan?

When people ask me where that country is, I begin by asking them some questions too. Have they heard for example of the Yellow River of China, that rises in the highlands of Kan-su and of Tibet, and then flows eastwards, joining the Pacific Ocean, not far from Peking? And have they heard of that classical river known as the Oxus which rises in the Pamir Mountains, or " The Roof of the World," as that region is sometimes spoken of, and flows westward to the Aral Sea? Having got such points

settled, I would explain that though the basins of the
Yellow River and of the Oxus are both on about the
same 40th parallel of N. latitude, yet there is a big
space between them—possibly 2,000 miles wide from
east to west. What is that space? It is just a third
basin—that of Lob Nor, but it has no outlet to any sea.
Chinese Turkestan is a part of the Lob basin—its
western half.

If one could get a bird's-eye view of the entire area
of it, it would probably have the appearance of an
elongated bowl, not at sea level, but fairly high up in
the world, flat at the bottom, and rising abruptly on
some of its sides, more especially on the south, the
west, and the north-west.

In reality here we have what once upon some
geological time was an inland sea quite as large as our
own Mediterranean, in the south of Europe. That
inland sea has dried up and disappeared; and to
remind us of its former existence, there is only its
sandy, and salt-encrusted bed, now a desert waste of
boundless extent, and in that waste a miniature survival from the past in the form of the reedy swamp of
Lob Nor. It is still the reservoir into which such
present-day rivers of Chinese Turkestan as can travel
so far through the thirsty sands discharge their
superfluous waters.

Much of this dry and arid region, whereon there is
hardly a vestige of vegetation, is girt by some of the
loftiest mountains in the world. On the south, three
successive ranges follow each other—the Nan-Shan,
the Kun-lun, and the Karakoram, acting as so many

buttresses to the high tablelands of Tibet and Ladakh ; on the west, the Pamirs, dividing the waters of the Oxus from those of the Kashgar and Yarkand rivers, within the Lob Nor drainage area ; and on the north-west, the Thian-Shan or Celestial Mountains : all are ranges snowclad on their summits, but dry and bare, and vegetationless lower down on the Chinese Turkestan side.

But where, it may be asked, amid such desolation are the human habitations ? There are to be found clinging to the mountains, just about where their outskirts touch the fringe of the central desert, or maybe meet the shore-line of the pre-historic sea, patches of vegetation, isolated from each other by dry and barren expanses of sand or gravel, but always situated close to some river or stream that has come down from the snowfields and glaciers in the higher regions. These patches are oases, and if they are green and fruitful it is only because man has made them so with the aid of his irrigation canals. There is no other way of bringing water to his fields, because practically no rain falls in Turkestan. The plains are in the rain-shadow of the mountains towering above them, and the crest of these intercepts any moisture that may come from the direction of the Indian, or the Arctic, Oceans.

The oases vary much in size. Some are large fortified towns, and others mere villages consisting of a few farmhouses. But, big or small, they all have the same characteristic of being situated at the foot of the mountains, and on the edge of the desert. I need not

weary my reader with a list of their names ; suffice it
to say that the most celebrated of them, in the direction of our own territory of Kashmir are Khotan,
Yarkand, and Kashgar—all ancient towns founded
by Buddhists, long before their conversion to Islamism
in the tenth century.

Though at the present time the country is so dry
that there is only enough water to supply the towns
and their cultivations, yet that may not have always
been so ; for recently the remains of habitations have
been discovered away in the desert, and deeply buried
in sand, while rows of dried-up trunks of poplar trees
and old river beds show where water used to flow.

Something has brought about a change. Some say
that the climate has become drier even since the
beginning of the Christian era, and with less water
coming down from the surrounding mountains many
places have dried up and consequently have had to be
abandoned. Others reject the climatic change theory,
and have another explanation just as ingenious.
According to them, the glaciers in the mountains,
from which the rivers down in the plains receive their
water, are enormous in size; in fact far too enormous
to be accounted for by the comparatively scanty snow
and rainfall of the present time. Therefore these
glaciers must have been relics of a former age, of some
glacial period for instance. None the less, big as they
are, they are nothing like as big as they once were,
owing to the melting that has gone on ; and, as a
consequence, the amount of water they now supply
to the rivers has correspondingly diminished. Paren-

thetically I may remark that if this theory be true, then
it seems that the water I have been drinking for so
many years in Kashgar was not what I thought it was
—the melted snow of a recent date, but melted ice of
some remote geological age.

It is worth noting that this is indeed a country of
mountains and plains. We have here in relatively
close proximity to each other some of the highest, and
some of the lowest spots on the whole of the earth's
surface. At the Kashgar end of Chinese Turkestan
the Tengri Nor in the Thian-Shan range rises to
24,000 feet, the Tagharma peak of the Pamir group,
to 25,146 feet, and in the Karakoram range, Mount
Godwin Austin—better known as K2—at 28,278 feet,
claims to be the second highest mountain in the world.
And yet in opposition to these snowy heights towering
above the level of the sea, a part of the oasis of Turfan
actually sinks to a depth of 1,000 feet below it, and in
consequence, the heat there in summer is so oppressive
that the natives are driven away from their ordinary
habitations to take refuge in caves.

But, whatever may have been the cause of the
abandonment of ancient habitations in the desert,
there can be no doubt about these sand-buried places
having been the means of preserving a mass of objects
of antiquarian interest.

As long ago as 1893, my husband acquired a
quantity of broken pottery, stone and metal seals, and
stucco figurines of Buddha, and some thirty-five leaves
of manuscripts—all things he bought in the bazaar
from native " treasure-seekers," evidently picked up

by them in the desert. He looked upon his acquisitions as so many curios ; nevertheless he sent them to the late Professor Hoernle, once a well-known Sanskrit scholar in Calcutta. What was his surprise when the Professor wrote to tell him that these manuscripts were the oldest Indian hand-written documents then known to exist : they were of the fourth century A.D.

Just before my husband came to Kashgar a British traveller—Captain Bower—had come across in Chinese Turkestan a manuscript book of remarkable antiquity. That caused the Russian Consul at Kashgar—Mons. N. Petrovsky—to be on the look-out, and, what with Mons. Petrovsky's finds, and those of my husband, Oriental scholars in Europe soon began to realize that this was a country offering a field for archæological research. Many scientific expeditions came in consequence, almost from every part of Europe and America, the most important of them being those of our friends, Sir Aurel Stein, and the late Professor von Le Coq. They excavated a great number of ruined sites around the Taklamakan Desert—often at several days' march from any present-day habitation.

And richly have their labours been rewarded. Among the things they have brought back are manuscripts in large quantities—written possibly in some twenty different languages. Those in Chinese, Tibetan, Sanskrit, Persian, Arabic, Syriac, etc., can, I suppose be read with more or less ease. But there are others in languages whose very names are unfamiliar to all but a few scholars engaged in research work. Who of us, for example, has heard of Sogdian, Central Asian

Brahmi, Manichæan, Uighur, Tanguti, Kuchean? The materials on which these scripts are written are as varied as the scripts themselves—for instance :—birch-bark, leather, silk cloth, wooden tablets, and paper.

And *à propos* of paper my readers will be interested to know that Sir Aurel Stein is the finder of the oldest specimen of that material in existence. He has a Chinese paper document which bears a date corresponding to the time when Christ was on earth.

The manuscripts range from the first to the eighth century A.D. They deal with all sorts of subjects—accounts, title deeds, official instructions, commercial letters, sepulchral inscriptions, Buddhist canons, and so on. But what will appeal most to our imagination is the discovery of scraps in a Syriac writing of the New Testament ; evidently relics of the Middle Ages when Chinese Turkestan had a fairly large population of Nestorian Christians.

Pictorial art in various forms is also well represented. Among the finds there are pictures of Buddhist monks and demoniac divinities, stucco reliefs, wall paintings from cave temples representing scenes in the life of Buddha, pieces of tapestry and embroidery, all of a high order of technique, showing, in many instances, different outside influences, such as Chinese, Indian, Persian, and Greek. Indeed, judging by its relics of the past, one would suppose that Turkestan had once had a highly developed civilization, and was also a sort of dumping ground for alien cultures. And all this, at a period when the Ancient Britons painted themselves with woad, and performed the horrid rite of human sacrifice in primeval oak forests !

If any of my readers think that I am making too much of the past cultural importance of Turkestan, let him or her go to the British Museum, ask for the " Stein Collection," and then judge for him or herself.

Chinese Turkestan, as the name implies, belongs to China, and is governed by the Chinese. To them the natives or Turkis are aliens, just as the Indians are to us in India.

Their connection with these Central Asian people dates as far back as the Han dynasty (202 B.C. to 220 A.D.). In the course of the intervening centuries their rule has been repeatedly obliterated and for long periods : but the prestige of the Chinese Empire has been so great that the Chinese always managed to come back, and this, not so much by force of arms, as through the willing submission of the natives themselves who seem to have greater faith in Chinese justice than in that of their own people.

The natives are Sunni Mohammedans. They are essentially docile and easily managed, with no strong characteristics either good or bad. The Chinese have a rather cynical saying about them—with which I do not quite agree—that they are insensible alike to kindness and to ill-treatment. Nor is the ruler's management of the ruled inconsistent with that not very flattering idea. There is nothing altruistic in the Chinese mode of government, the object of which is to keep an outward appearance of law and order, and, at the same time, to levy such taxes as are possible for the maintenance of the administration. Apart from that I should say that on the whole the Chinese are rather callous as to the well-being of the natives. At the same time they do not go out of their way to irritate them by the making of laws, for instance, calculated to make people happy in spite of themselves.

Though the Chinese are Confucians, they avoid all interference with the religious and social life of the natives, and what intercourse the Chinese Amban has with the people over whom he rules is mostly through native begs or headmen. These may, with impunity, practise a certain amount of oppression on their fellow countrymen, and so long as this is not carried to excess the Chinese do not interfere. There is one principle of government which they seem to understand better than we mostly do, namely, that if you want to keep a country quiet it is less advantageous to you to have the common people contented than to have the influential ones among them on your side : in other words, keep the shepherds pleased, and never mind about the sheep, because they are dumb !

The language of the country is Jagatai Turki, which is of the same family as the Turkish of Constantinople, and is probably a purer Turkish, for it has not become so mixed up with other tongues, such as Persian and Arabic. Turki is decidedly complicated, with its 29,000 possible tenses !

Politically Chinese Turkestan is of some interest to us Britishers. In the first place it borders on our territory of Kashmir, and, despite the difficulties of communication across the Himalayas, there is a considerable colony of British-Indian merchants at Yarkand and Kashgar always travelling to and fro with their horse caravans laden in one direction with Indian spices and Manchester cotton prints, and in the other with Turkestan merchandise such as gold, jade, Khotan carpets, Kirghiz felts, and, above all, a narcotic extracted from the hemp plant (*Cannabis sativa*), and known in India as Bhang or Cheras, in Turkestan as Nasha, and to us in Europe as Hashish.

But, apart from these considerations, Chinese Turkestan, or rather the south-western part of it, is, like Afghanistan, on that belt of foreign countries which insulates India from contact with Russia in Central Asia ; and as Russia was continually pushing her border towards the south, it was a matter of concern to us that the *status quo* of those insulating countries, or buffer states should be maintained. Although there was no occasion to suspect the Russian Government of any design on India, yet there was a war party in the country amongst the military officers—a party that would be glad of any occasion for filibustering if it led to a shower of decorations. The Russian Bear has a small tail, but that tail often wags the head ! And so it was necessary to have someone on the watch.

My husband first went to Kashgar in 1890 with Captain (now Sir Francis) Younghusband, who even then was famous as a traveller. Many years have passed since then, but my husband is never tired of going over his happy reminiscences of the time when he and Captain Younghusband travelled about the

Pamirs together; and of the evenings he spent, chronometer watch in hand, acting as time-keeper, while Captain Younghusband took his astronomical observations for latitude before they turned into their smoky Kirghiz tent to play their nightly game of draughts.

When Captain Younghusband returned to India in the following year, my husband was told to remain in Chinese Turkestan for the double purpose of looking after the British traders, and of keeping an eye on the Russian activities in the direction of our Kashmir border.

It need hardly be said that he was anything but a *persona grata* with the Russian Consulate at Kashgar, and for many years—indeed from 1890 to 1907—he met with a good deal of opposition from that quarter. The Chinese were very much under the thumb of the Russians, and, although my husband always had extremely pleasant relations with the Chinese, yet at a certain period of his stay in Kashgar his position was hardly tenable in the face of Russian attempts to force the Chinese to turn him out of the country. Certainly, but for the fact that my husband's father was secretary to the Chinese Legation in London, and my husband had been recommended to the kind attention of the Tao-tai of Kashgar by the Chinese Minister in London, the probability was that he would have had to leave the country.

The year 1907 was, however, a turning point in my husband's position. In that year Sir Arthur Nicholson, afterwards Lord Carnock, then British Ambassador in St. Petersburg, made a treaty with the Russian Government concerning certain problems connected with Persia, Afghanistan and Tibet. This treaty apparently brought about a *rapprochement* between England and Russia, and for the time being we were not thwarted in the usual way by the Russians in whatever we tried to do in Asia. Though Sir Arthur Nicholson probably never had Kashgar in his mind when he signed that treaty, yet the British Agent at that place did receive some benefit from it. For the Russian Consulate suddenly ceased its hostile attitude towards him, and in 1908 the British Government were able to get the Chinese to agree—what we did not succeed in doing before, owing to Russian opposition—to my husband being appointed British Consul, and two years later, Consul-General.

CHAPTER V

THE MOHAMMEDAN, OR OLD CITY OF KASHGAR

THERE are two Kashgar cities, the one being the old, or Mohammedan City, with about 40,000 inhabitants, mostly Mohammedans, though the Chinese Civil Administration is carried on there. The Tao-tai, a personage with a rank corresponding more or less to that of a Commissioner in India, is at the head, and is assisted by a District Officer known as the Hsien-Kuan. And, as there are a Russian, and a British Consulate at Kashgar, he has a special Assistant called the Tung-shang, whose duty it is to treat affairs with the Consuls.

The Ti-tai, who is a sort of Provincial Commander-in-Chief, has his residence in the Chinese New City, where most of the troops are kept, though a small quota is quartered in the Old City, commanded by a Hsie-tai, or Colonel.

The New City is seven miles to the South of the Old, and is smaller; the population being almost entirely Chinese. Both cities are walled in by enormously thick crenellated walls, in which are four massive iron gates, which are shut at sunset, and opened at daybreak, to the blowing of horns and firing of guns. And both cities are surrounded by wide moats, which look imposing, though I don't believe they are ever filled. Probably if they were, the water would melt the foundations of the wall, which seem to be simply of mud or of unbaked brick.

The two Consulates, and later the Russo-Asiatic Bank, and the Swedish Mission Station, were outside the wall of the Old City, though eventually the Swedes established a Mission station in the New City, to work among the Chinese.

The streets of the Mohammedan City were very narrow and dirty, with the ground all ups and downs, and mostly muddy from the water slopped over from the pails of the donkeys and water carriers. Dark little shops lined the streets, in some places made darker by the covering or awning of reed mats that was erected right across the road for shade. The shop-keepers squatted in the midst of their goods, and never seemed particularly anxious for customers.

Just inside the gate, and along the street leading to the central bazaar, the beggars congregated, and most horrible sights many of them were, with their faces and limbs eaten away and distorted with the most frightful diseases.

The narrow bazaars seemed to be always crowded, and especially so on Thursdays, the Bazaar-Kun, or Market Day. Then it was a slow business to push one's way through the throng of people, some on foot, others mounted on donkeys and horses, animals so loaded with fodder that only a nose and four hoofs could be seen, and caravans of camels and horses, carrying great hard bales of cotton. The bells the camels wore always sounded to me so like a peal of church bells that sometimes on a Sunday morning, when sitting in the garden, hearing the camels down at the river, I closed my eyes and felt as though I was at home and it was church time.

The main streets seemed mostly to run into the big Market Square known as the Id-ga, in the centre of which stood the Chief Mosque. On Friday morning all the men went there, dressed in their best, to say their prayers, and from the roof of this Mosque we heard from our house at intervals during the day, the Mullah's call to prayer. I always loved to hear their musical voices intoning : " Allah-ho-Akbar "—" God is Great," but the time it thrilled me most was when I was sometimes wakened at the dawn of a beautiful summer morning, to hear the call to the Faithful floating away over the country through the still cool air.

I wish I could adequately describe the beauty and picturesqueness of the Id-ga bazaar, as seen from the steps of the Mosque. In the centre of the great square were the fruit stalls ; in summer piled high with fruit, crimson peaches, apricots, mulberries, enormous bunches of black and white grapes and purple and yellow figs. One kind of white grape had berries about two inches long, and as thick as one's finger. Then there were melons of so many varieties, some being cut open to show the inside. Enormous water melons, almost too heavy to lift, with their red flesh and black seeds ; melons green all through, and intensely sweet; melons with pink insides; and others pure white, or apricot-coloured when cut open. Fruit in Kashgar was too cheap to be appreciated. A huge melon cost about twopence. Peaches and apricots perhaps a halfpenny a pound, grapes about a shilling a donkey load. We never gave dessert at a dinner party, for it was altogether too cheap and commonplace.

Then the Cap stalls gave a wonderfully pretty touch of colour. They looked like flowers on their stands. Bright coloured velvet caps of every hue, some lined and trimmed with fur for winter, others gaily embroidered for summer wear, and round which a turban could be wound for full dress; and some decorated with patterns of silver beaten thin and sewn on : these were for the women to wear on high days and holidays.

The people too were all dressed in the brightest of colours; and a Kashgar crowd was very gay compared with an English one. The brilliant shades suited them and their surroundings so perfectly.

The side streets were often given up to one special trade, and so you found the Cotton bazaar, the Chintz bazaar, where the Russian prints were sold, the Blacksmiths' and the Silversmiths' bazaars, the flour and grain bazaars, and so on. And one horrible place went by the name of the flea bazaar, for it was there that the old clothes were sold, and I am pretty certain that it lived up to its name.

Of course, the inevitable tea shop, or Chai-Khana, was everywhere, where people sat and drank tea while they listened to dreamy native music played by a band consisting of perhaps one or two long-necked mando-line-shaped instruments that produced very soft fairy-like music, accompanied by a small drum. Or they listened to a professional story teller. He was a very fascinating person to watch, and I often wished I could understand what he was saying. He lost himself so completely in the story he was telling that he held his audience spellbound, while he acted the thrilling deeds he was relating. I suppose it was just this way that the Arabian Nights romances were first told.

Many of the shops had a wicker birdcage hanging up, in which was a red-legged partridge, called a Kek-lik, so named for the sound he made, or a ground lark which sang continually a shrill, trilling song. I have often thought that a good musician could write a fine symphony, inspired by the sounds of the city, with the chatter of the people, the thud of hoofs, the not unmusical screech of the great wooden wheels of the native carts, and the melodious camel bells, as an accompaniment to the songs of the little imprisoned larks.

The people of Kashgar are of many different types. Tall, handsome, aristocratic-looking men and women, with almost European features, rosy-cheeked and flat-faced people of the Kirghiz type, Afghans with their thin, sharp profiles, natives of India, both Hindu and Mohammedan, and Chinese. One met too, fair-haired and blue-eyed people, showing possibly their unmixed Aryan descent. One could hardly say what the real Kashgar type was, for it has become so mixed by the invasion of other peoples in the past. Many of the women were very attractive, and some of the children extraordinarily handsome, especially the dark-eyed boys and girls of about twelve, who looked quite Italian or Spanish in their velvet coats and tight-fitting caps.

The Kashgar crowd is a very happy, peaceable one. Everyone seems to be contented and gay, and life goes easily. The Kashgari lives a simple, quiet life, and his wants are few. He is a placid individual, except when he is roused to a wordy argument over a bargain. Then he tells the other party very fluently what he thinks of him, and that he is no good Mussulman, or when he really has a serious quarrel about a woman, or over the question of water for his fields.

The men's costume consists of a white shirt and white baggy trousers, over which a long coloured coat is worn in hot weather, or in winter several padded coats, one put on top of the other. The coats are made of red native cotton cloth called *kham*, Russian printed chintz, or velvet. In very cold weather, or for travelling, a sheepskin coat, with the fur turned inside, is a satisfactory protection, though it may be neither beautiful nor hygienic. Men and boys have their heads shaved, and they always wear a cap of some description, it being considered rather a disgrace to be seen with the head uncovered : men, women, and children and even small babies sleep with their caps on. The caps are made of velvet, lined and edged with fur for winter, while small embroidered skull caps are worn in summer. Turbans are the headgear of the mullahs and rich merchants, except at the time of the Great Ramazan feast, when men of all classes don them, and even small boys walk about proudly in their best velvet coats, with the imposing white headdress.

A man is never seen without a belt, which is made either of yards of muslin, wound many times round the waist; a bright-coloured handkerchief, with embroidered corners, tied in a knot in front with one embroidered corner carefully arranged to hang in the centre of the back; or of a wide band of embroidery fastened with a great silver buckle. To the belt is always attached the snuff bottle, and mostly a knife in a sheath: and the clothes being firmly held in round the waist by the belt make a useful receptacle when one is shopping. Purchases are all stuffed down inside the shirt, even meat and food.

One day my cook came home from the bazaar with a very portly figure and one that seemed to be moving and bulging out in strange places. I watched him unburden himself of his purchases in the kitchen, and to my surprise, there came out a weird collection of things that reminded me of a conjurer's trick. First of all he pulled out his day's supply of native bread cakes, then some vegetables and meat, various small packages in paper, and lastly one by one, six live pigeons he had bought to make into a pie for our dinner.

Our servants were always very keen to have my husband's cast-off clothes, but when I found that they insisted on wearing the shirt outside the trousers, hanging down below the jacket, I had to insist on native clothing being worn in the house !

The boots reach to the knee, the upper part and feet being of soft leather, with loose over-shoes that are only put on out of doors, and are left on the doorstep when entering a house. Inside the boots, felt stockings are worn.

The women dress in very much the same way as the men, excepting that the under dress and long wide trousers are mostly of coloured material and, in the case of rich women, are of embroidered silk. They wear a little bright-coloured waistcoat edged with gold brocade and over it a short jacket also very much decorated. This constitutes the indoor dress. For going out, a long coat reaching to the heels is put on, made of velvet, silk, or chintz, as the case may be. These coats are very similar to those worn by the men, only they are longer and have bands of brocade on the chest to denote, by their number, the standing of the wearer, whether she is single, newly married, or a matron with a family. But no belt is ever worn, being considered indecent for a woman. The caps are much like the men's generally, though for full outdoor dress some of the older women wear huge pork-pie shaped hats, with broad bands of fur turned up all round. Over everything, hat and all, a big white muslin coat is thrown, and held together in front with the sleeves, through which the arms are never put, hanging down behind. A thick veil made of cotton material beautifully worked all over in a pattern of drawn thread work, is worn down over the face, or thrown back over the cap or hat. Some women were very particular to keep their veils down, but I always suspected that it was the plain ones who were so modest, while the pretty ones did not want to hide their charms. And many of the young women and girls looked really charming, with a bright marigold, a zenia, or a scarlet pomegranate flower tucked over the ear to give a finishing touch to the toilette. They mixed up the most glaring colours quite indiscriminately, but somehow they never seemed to clash on the fair wearers.

The boots for ordinary occasions, worn by the women were like the men's; but for smart wear they went in for abnormally high heels, sometimes of coloured leather, with patterns of the same leather up the back of the leg.

The hair is worn parted in the middle, and is always jet black; fair hair and eyes being not at all admired. It is plaited into long pigtails, that are made up and lengthened with yâk's hair, till they reach nearly to the knees. The number of plaits worn also shows the wearer's standing, girls having many little thin ones, while, as they advance in years, so the number decreases, and the size of the plait increases, until a portly matron has only two very thick ones, beautifully black, and shiny, and quite stiff with some gluey stuff; as a woman only has her hair done for great occasions, it is necessary to stiffen it to keep it glossy and tidy. The long hair which looks so smart and well kept is, in reality, in a most horribly dirty condition, positively alive with vermin; and that was one important reason why I never felt I could have a woman to wait on me.

One of the Missionaries told us how, one day, when for some reason he could not see his out-patients in the dispensary, he took into his own room some women and children. They would sit leaning their heads against his bed, so he told them not to, as he did not want live things left in his bed. One woman turned to another, who had not understood what was said, and shouted at her : " He says there are live things in his bed and we shall get them," and up they all jumped. It had the desired effect, but was not exactly what our friend had meant.

The Kashgaris of both sexes wear their sleeves quite six inches below the hands, and to do anything these sleeves must be rolled up to get the hands free.

It was very funny to see two men make a bargain to sell and buy a horse or cow, or anything that meant a big deal. They went up to each other, holding out the right hand which they put up each other's sleeve. Then some mystic sign, such as putting out the number of fingers that would indicate the price offered, or tapping each other's arm so many times, passed between them. I never could quite discover what they did. But these two stood linked together, gazing into each other's faces and solemnly shaking or nodding their heads, until the price was decided upon. Then they withdrew their hands, stroked their beards, and after a little money had passed between them the transaction was complete. And all had been done quite secretly, though probably a crowd had been watching them.

The long sleeves had many uses, as a muff in cold weather, as a handkerchief, or a duster, and when a Kashgari wanted to show contempt, or disgust, he put his nose into the opening of the sleeve. Once or twice women have done that in passing us, but not often, I am glad to say. They more often salaamed, and the men dismounted in passing us, sometimes even pressing us to take their horses if we were walking. They never could understand why we went on foot when there were horses standing in the stables. Only poor people who could not afford even a donkey, ever walked anywhere.

To keep the hands covered was a sign of respect, and one should never show one's hands before a superior unless they were being used.

When I first went to Kashgar, very little foreign material had been brought to the bazaar, and everyone, except a few very rich bais, who always went clad in velvet, was dressed in their native red *kham*. Practically no Russian stores were to be found, and sugar was scarce. It was rather wonderful to think that the City, with its streets and bazaars, looked just as it must have done for centuries, and the people were living and dressing in very much the same fashion as did their forefathers. Our mode of travelling, too, was just the same as it had been in the days when Marco Polo passed through these parts on his way to the Court of Kublai-Khan in the thirteenth century.

Very soon, however, after I arrived a great change began to take place. Materials, stores, utensils, household furniture and fittings, sugar, and white flour were brought by caravan from Russia and India. The rich merchants began building Europeanized houses, using chairs and tables, and even the common people dressed in gaudy, large-patterned Russian prints, mostly with hideous pink roses scattered about a bright background.

But I was much surprised when, soon after I arrived, I sent a man to buy me a reel of white cotton, and he brought home one with the familiar name of " Coats " on it in Russian. Singer sewing machines were used by the tailors and looked somehow rather out of place when used by a man sitting on his heels in a dark little shop in a narrow bazaar.

My first walk through the city was a great experience. As we were approaching the gate nearest to our house, we came to a wide puddle in the road. I was preparing to jump over it when a wizened old Chinaman came along, with a basket on his back. He bowed low to us, put his basket into the puddle, and held out his hand gallantly to help me step on it, and over to dry ground. I was quite touched by his kind thought, and the graceful way he did it all. And he made it quite evident that it was not done in the hope of a *bukhshish.*

The fun began when I got into the bazaar ; crowds gathered round us ; women and children tried to stroke my coat and dress, and to peer into my face, till at last we simply could not move. They were not hostile at all, but curious and interested, and all the time called us " Feranghis " or " Franks." But it was too much for me. We managed to squeeze into a shop, and the owner at once brought us tea and sweets. The people tried to crowd in too, but our servants who were with us managed to disperse them, and we got home later by some back streets.

It was long before I ventured into the city again, though, before I left Kashgar for good, I could walk through the bazaars alone, and very little notice was taken of me. European women had become by that time too ordinary for people to bother about.

One day, walking in the country, we were followed by two men, who began discussing what I was. One said I could not be a woman, because I wore a belt; the other replied that I might be a man, because I did not show my trousers and had no hair, but they both agreed that I looked like a woman, as I had no beard. Evidently I was just a great puzzle to them.

One day a little urchin ran in front of me, and looking up in my face remarked : " Just like a monkey." He made himself scarce pretty quickly.

CHAPTER VI

THE CHINESE, OR NEW CITY, AND A
CHINESE DINNER

ONE day invitations arrived for us from the Ti-tai and his wife to a Chinese dinner in the New City.

It was to be a first class banquet, that is to say, one that included both swallow's - nest soup and sucking-pig. The invitations were in the form of a long strip of red paper, about two feet long and six inches wide, folded backwards, and forwards, and placed in a red envelope. Some tiny characters were written on the invitation that in English would read something like this: "Respectfully, with goblet in hand, I await the light of your countenance on the sixth day of the first moon at midday." As we accepted we kept the documents to show that we did so.

If it had been a dinner of the second class we were invited to, that is, one at which sucking-pig would be served, but not swallow's nest, the invitations would have been written on a small red card, with a list of the guests on it. Each one invited would have written beside his name something in very flowery language to the effect that he accepted or refused, and have returned the card to the messenger who brought it.

But we were to be honoured with the very best

of entertainments, and I was quite excited at the prospect.

As the time was fixed for midday, we were obliged to make an early start, for I wanted to see something of the Chinese city ; and I innocently thought it would be less fatiguing to do the seven miles in a Chinese cart than on horseback, and also I knew that crackers would be let off in salute as we entered the Ti-tai's *yamên*. I did not at all like the idea of being on horseback at that moment, and thought that a Chinese mule would be accustomed to such shocks. So we hired a Chinese " Marpa." It looked so neat and smart when it drove up, with a fine mule in the shafts. The cart was box-shaped, with a rounded top, the sides being a kind of trellis work, lined with blue material, decorated with an appliqué of black velvet. There was a curtain that could be let down in front for the privacy of modest ladies. These carts can be hired anywhere and are the public cabs of the Chinese. There were no springs, and the body rested directly on the axle between two large wooden wheels ; and like everything else Chinese was painted red ; red being their lucky colour.

Our servants put in a lot of rugs and pillows for padding, and I got in, thinking I was going to have a delightful drive. But I was undeceived as soon as we got out on the main road, where there was a sharp rise up to an irrigation canal. My driver jumped off his perch on the shafts and, running along beside the cart, whipped up the mule, which rushed full speed to the top of the hill, crossed the canal slanting-wise, so letting down first one wheel then the other with most alarming bumpings and swayings, throwing me about helplessly from side to side ; then the driver nimbly jumped back on to the shafts, and away we went full tilt down the hill while I put my hat straight and felt for broken bones. And so we went round outside the city wall to the jingle of the bells hung round the mule's neck and the musical cries of the driver, or "Marpa-kesh." He sat there on the shafts, thumping the old mule just above her tail, making all sorts of funny noises to direct her and cheer her on. The driving was done entirely by the voice, for there were no reins, nor bit, only a rope from the animal's head.

The driver was quite an acrobat in the way he hopped off his seat when we came to a specially difficult or broken bit of road, and on again without slowing down. But as the Kashgar roads are all holes, and steps, and ankle deep in dust, to go far over them in a springless cart is well nigh torture after a very short time.

Leaving the Old City behind us, we crossed the river by a very dilapidated bridge, which was full of holes, and found ourselves on the New City Road, a fine wide avenue of poplar and willow trees, along which a stream of people on horses, and donkeys, and in carts, were also wending their way to the Chinese City.

At last to my great relief we came to signs of Chinese habitations, and saw Chinamen working in the fields, and almost at once we got a sight of the city wall, with a pagoda perched upon it. In a few minutes we were in a crowded bazaar, which led to the gate through which we drove, and found ourselves inside the New City, with Chinese soldiers crowding round to see us.

It was quite different from the Old City, being smaller, and newer looking. Chinese shops lined the streets; the restaurants, such as they were, were full of Chinese soldiers in their blue padded cotton clothes, and with black scarves round their heads.

We stopped at the biggest shop and were quite gushingly received by the owner, who took us into his private room, and insisted on giving us tea. He brought out rolls of beautiful silk brocade, many in lovely pale colours, and artistic patterns, fascinating jade ornaments in neat little boxes with glass sides, trinkets and head dresses made of kingfisher feathers, coral, china, great cloisonné vases, bowls, teapots, etc., etc. A fascinating array but all at very exorbitant prices.

These merchants in Kashgar are from Tientsin, and besides trading and keeping a shop, they are bankers and moneylenders, and are always out to drive a very hard bargain with anyone they deal with; one minute they treat you as a dearest friend, and the next try their utmost to swindle you, all the time with the friendliest smile on their faces.

After a lot of good-natured haggling, we managed to buy a few odds and ends, but it was so difficult to know what was a reasonable price to pay for anything. Even food and household necessities had to be bought in this very unsatisfactory way, and there was no fixed price for anything. It would have been impossible for me to do any household shopping, for prices would have gone up a hundredfold as soon as I appeared. The only way was to depute one of the servants to do all the buying.

But as time was going, we could not loiter among these lovely things, or we would be late for our dinner party.

We drove on through narrow, winding streets, with Chinese soldiers and highly-painted native women staring at us, past the temple, in which was also the theatre, until we arrived outside the gate of the *yamên*. What struck me most was the tawdriness and shabbiness of the whole city ; there did not seem to be a good building in it, not even the temple and theatre.

A man had been sent out to meet us and had galloped back to give warning of our arrival to those deputed to let off the horrid crackers. As we went through the gate, bang went the salutes. All the horses reared and danced about, and I was so thankful that I was behind a steady old mule which was quite accustomed to such greetings.

Outside the door of the house was a wall or screen, with a vicious-looking dragon painted on it. All Chinese houses and temples have this screen outside the door to prevent the evil spirits entering the house, because an evil spirit can only walk straight ahead, and cannot turn round a corner, and so is stopped by this screen. We went round it safely and found ourselves in a big courtyard, with the Ti-tai and his lady coming to meet us and walk hand in hand with us to the front door.

Of course, my husband and I were taken to different parts of the house, and did not meet again until after all was over and we were leaving the *yamên*; so I was greatly relieved to find that the two Swedish ladies were also invited, for they would at least be able to speak to the servants in Turki and possibly some of the Chinese ladies would know something of the native language. There were also several Chinese lady guests.

We were taken into a large, simply-furnished room. At one end was the *kang* or platform raised about three feet from the ground; to this my hostess led me. It was built of brick, like a huge oven, and in winter was heated by fire being put inside. On it were red mats and bolster-like cushions, for it was the sleeping place at night, and in the day the seat of honour for guests. A small table about a foot high was placed towards the front of the *kang*, and my hostess and I took our seats, one each side of it, I being on my hostess's left hand, with cups of tea on the table between us. And a very warm seat it was too !

In the other part of the room were some high square tables and high, uncomfortable rectangular chairs to match, with thin cushions on the seats. Everything was red—the furniture of a dark shade, and the cushions brighter. On the walls were two or three scrolls, and on stands some beautiful vases.

The windows were of a fancy lattice work, covered with paper.

Everyone was very friendly and crowded round me, the newcomer, to see how I was dressed. They opened my fur coat to see what I wore beneath it, stroked the feather in my hat, and seemed highly amused at my serviceable winter clothing. My black shoes and stockings caused quite an excitement, and I am afraid were not admired. The little ladies put out their tiny embroidered satin shoes to compare with them, and went into peals of laughter a mine, till I tucked them away under me, hoping they would forget all about the ugly black things. I began to feel so embarrassed, and was much relieved when dinner was announced.

Our hostess led me to my place on her left hand, and taking a tiny wine cup from a servant, raised it to her forehead before placing it on the table before my chair. Then she went through the same ceremony with a pair of chopsticks; she shook my chair to make certain that it would bear me, and passed her sleeve over the seat to brush away the dust. This performance had to be gone through for each guest before we could sit down.

We sat round a big square table on which were a number of small bowls containing sauces and condiments; then the serving began. We started with ancient eggs that had been buried in lime for a very long time; they were not as bad as I expected they would be, and when one tried to imagine that they were what they very much resembled, gorgonzola cheese, and not bad eggs, they were quite possible to eat. Then followed about forty courses—meat, vegetables, poultry, dried fish of many kinds, sea slugs, ducks, shark's fins, seaweed, lotus seeds, and roots, fungi of various sorts, sweet dishes, and the very special delicacies, sucking-pig, which seemed to be simply the crackling served sweet, and swallow's nest soup. Everything was cut into small pieces, for convenience of eating with chopsticks, I suppose.

I was very curious to see, and try, the swallow's-nest soup I had heard so much about, but I was quite disappointed in it. It tasted just as though it had been made with vermicelli, highly flavoured with onion and garlic, and I could not find anything very delicious about it whatever. It is made from the gelatinous lining of the nest of a special breed of swallow that lives in the south of China and builds in most inaccessible places on the cliffs. The nest lining is about the size of half a tablespoon ; one side, where it has been stuck against the cliff, being cut off just like a spoon cut in half. It is very beautifully made, and looks like fine vermicelli woven into a tiny basket. The idea is not a very nice one, I know, but it seems that the birds themselves make this gelatinous stuff with their saliva to line their little nests.

At a dinner of men, this great dish must be honoured by being eaten with hats on ; and before it is put on the table, the servant of each guest brings his master's hat to him. As we were all wearing our hats, no difference was made ; and perhaps mere womenfolk are not expected to observe all these niceties of etiquette.

All through the long meal a servant kept coming round with a kettle of boiling spirit to replenish the wine cups, and I am afraid we rather gave offence by not drinking it.

Another servant wandered about with a very greasy-looking wet cloth, ready to wipe anyone's hands and face who needed the attention. Needless to say I did not make use of him !

It is as well that the table had an upstanding edge all round, for most of the dishes were served in soup or gravy, which slopped over the bowls and dripped off the dainty morsels as they were being conveyed about by the chopsticks.

We found on the table in our places, besides the chopsticks, knives, forks and spoons. When I took up mine, to my surprise, I found they were my own and wondered how they had got there. Afterwards I learned that the Ti-tai had most thoughtfully sent a servant to suggest to Jafar Ali that he should bring a supply with him, and Jafar Ali had sensibly brought a cruet too. I tried valiantly to use the chopsticks and provided much amusement for the company ; nothing got as far as my mouth, for if I managed to pick up a bit of something from the bowl after long, patient efforts, I promptly dropped it on the table.

To the Chinese guests the dinner was most recherché. Many of the things had come from China and were very costly. But I found it difficult to swallow some of them, in spite of the mustard and salt Jafar Ali had provided. Any very dainty titbit my hostess insisted on my eating, conveying the choicest bits from the bowl with her own chopsticks to my mouth. I managed pretty well till the sea slugs came along : if they had been minced or disguised in some way, they might not have been so bad, but they were served boiled whole, and when I saw these huge black slugs, covered with lumps, wobbling about in front of me, I wondered how I should live through the ordeal of swallowing one. But there was no getting out of it and I was faced with the choice of eating it or giving offence. So I covered one well with mustard, shut my eyes, and swallowed it whole. The ladies were so pleased with me that they insisted on me eating another ; and three or four times I had to go through the awful ordeal. It was many days before I forgot those sea slugs, for eating the tough, gelatinous things whole like that made me horribly ill afterwards.

One little lady, seeing us apparently enjoying mustard, insisted on trying it ; we warned her to be careful, but she took a spoonful and put it in her mouth ; then there was a scene better imagined than described !

But, oh ! I did get tired, and how I longed for the cup of tea to appear which would be the signal for us to go ; we sat there from twelve till past five, and my head ached violently.

The Ti-tai and his wife escorted us again to the gate and we took an elaborate farewell. Again the nerve-wracking salute was fired, and again I bumped along in that awful cart, reaching home a complete wreck for the time being.

The polite thing to say to the host who has entertained you when you see him after a week or so is : " The taste of your dinner is still in my mouth." I could have said that with great feeling and perfect truth !

CHAPTER VII

HOUSEKEEPING DIFFICULTIES

I SOON settled down to my new life in a strange land, where manners and customs must be learnt from the beginning, and all one's ideas of housekeeping completely changed.

During my first period of over four years, I experienced to the very utmost what homesickness and loneliness meant. At first the language difficulty made me feel so cut off, and isolated, and to demoralize me still more, I had nothing whatever to claim my individual attention. All our clothes were new and in good condition, and sometimes I was tempted to cut holes in them that I might be obliged to sew them up. Our library was very limited, and materials could not be got for any sort of handwork that would interest me. And nothing seemed worth while doing, so utterly slack did I become. My husband was always very busy with his work and I saw him only at meal times, or when we had our constitutional in the afternoons ; and I soon felt I hated the people who were coming at all times bringing him petitions, and who must be attended to at once. So I was quite reconciled when our Indian cook declared that he must return to his home and people, and there was no one else to be found who knew anything whatever about English cooking.

I at once got another room made into a kitchen, with good windows that could be opened and a door large enough to go through without having to stoop, and clean whitewashed walls. Mr. Högberg made me a splendid little kitchener out of some old paraffin oil tins, and I became cook, with Isa Akhun as kitchen-boy and pupil.

Isa was a Kashgari and only knew about as much Hindustani as I did, but we made up a wonderful language of our own out of Turki, Hindustani, and English, and we understood each other quite well. And after all what more does one expect of the most perfectly spoken language ?

Our first business was to get good yeast bread made, instead of living on baking-powder rolls that we had got so tired of; and, after a few experiments and failures, we produced quite good light loaves of which I was inordinately proud. Isa was soon able to do the kneading, which was the heavy work of bread making.

We bought cream from the bazaar and made butter by shaking the cream in a big wide-mouthed bottle I begged from the Hospital Assistant. Isa, who loved a job he could just go on with quietly without having to use his brains too much, would sit patiently in front of the fire in winter, or on the doorstep in summer for hours, shaking this old bottle till the butter came; then we made cakes and pastry with it.

All the while I was learning Turki and Hindustani, and having practice in speaking. Our servants were very mixed as to nationality, and we had at times Kashgaris, Punjabis, Kashmiris, Ladakhis and Tibetans, a Cingalese, and once a Chinaman. But they all spoke Hindustani or Turki. The Chinaman was not a success, for the Chinese in Kashgar were not of the servant class, and looked upon themselves as " sahibs " and were quite above doing any work. This particular man refused to show me any respect, because I did cooking in the kitchen. He argued that our governess was a real lady because she read, and wrote all day, and taught the children, but the Memsahib did cooking and could not be a lady ; and he refused to serve me first at meals, or to take any orders from me.

I got on splendidly with my staff of men, and it was rarely that I had any trouble ; I found that they were just like children to manage. My first attempt at scolding in a foreign language was quite a failure, and it was long before I dare try again. I worked myself up to such a pitch of indignation and then felt an utter fool, when at the climax I had no word with which to express myself, and the man I was scolding sweetly supplied it to me. So I kept to English when my temper got the better of me, and found it was far more efficacious, for the culprit imagined that I was saying something much worse than I really was. I had read of a missionary who found great relief to his feelings by saying the alphabet very quickly backwards, and forwards, putting in effective accentuation here and there : I tried it once, but it sounded so comical to me that I laughed, and the charm was broken.

Poor Isa had tried hard to learn our ways, but it was uphill work, for the native cooking is so different from ours. I trained him for many years, but his mind would never run beyond a rice pudding. If you asked him what sweet he would make for dinner, he would look all over the ceiling, along the floor, into every corner of the room, as though selecting something very novel from his many recipes, and solemnly announce " rice pudding," the very word you had been expecting all the time. The natives could not begin a word with certain consonants and always tacked on a vowel first : so, sponge cake was " espongee-cake ; " frying-pan, " erfrilly-pan ; " plum pudding, " pullum-pud-ding ; " champagne, " esimp-kin ; " fritters, " perlitters " ; and I am afraid we caught the infection and pronounced these words in the same funny way.

Cooking in Kashgar meant a great deal more work than it does at home, for everything must be prepared from the very beginning. To make a cake, for instance, cream must be bought, and made into butter ; flour sifted and dried ; sugar pounded in a mortar and sifted ; almonds shelled, blanched and pounded, etc., before the real cake making began. And so with everything.

I began by making yeast from potatoes, and afterwards kept it going by putting away a lump of dough to be used as yeast for the next baking, and it answered fairly well until our first visitor came from India, Colonel (now Sir Henry) Powell, of the Gurkha Rifles. Of course, just because I wanted my bread to be specially good, the yeast went off for some reason and the bread was heavy. Colonel Powell was an expert in household matters, and he offered to show me how to make yeast from ground rice, sugar, and warm water. He made a concoction and put it into a champagne bottle; tied the cork firmly down; and put the bottle into a niche beside the Russian stove in the dining-room, to be left to ferment for two days. I got ready a basin of warm flour, and after dinner on the second day Colonel Powell said he would open the bottle for me to see if the yeast was in good condition. He cut the string and up shot the cork to the ceiling, with all the yeast after it, and down it poured on our heads like a thunder shower. Oh! the mess we were in, with the sticky fluid all over us! We had literally to scrape ourselves and each other, while we became feeble with laughing. So the yeast had to be made again, and left for another two days, but in a cooler place this time.

We very soon found that we must keep a cow of our own, for the milk from the bazaar had such an unpleasant taste. The natives would mix sheep's milk with cow's, and the horrible flavour of the sheep could not be covered by the strongest tea or coffee. We started with one cow, and, as our family increased, our number of cows did also, until we had three. Kashgar cows never give more than ten to twelve pints of milk in the twenty-four hours, and we needed a good deal to keep us in butter for the table.

Isa proved himself to be a splendid dairyman, though he had not learnt the art of soothing the animals before milking time like one of the men I had later, when Isa had been promoted to the work of carrying our mails.

This man used to sit and sing a gentle lullaby to the cows, and was convinced that the quantity and quality of their milk were improved by so doing.

Cows in Kashgar were never milked without their calves being present. In fact, a cow would not give a drop of milk until her baby had had the first pull, and was then allowed to stand where she could lick and fondle it, while the milking business was going on ; after which for an hour or two they were left together and the cow was sure to be milked dry. The Kash-garis have the idea that it is a sin against Nature to separate the cow from the calf, and perhaps they are not far wrong ; but there sometimes arose complications with their system, for if the calf died the cow was useless.

One of our calves died at a very early age, and not a drop of milk could we get ; so one of the men had the brilliant idea of skinning and stuffing the poor little beast. This was done in great haste, and a most frightful-looking creature was the result ; its legs were made of sticks, which stuck out in all directions, and straw peeped out of its eyes, and nose. I hated to look at it, and was sure the poor mother would not own it. But the silly old thing was overjoyed to get her lost infant back ; she smelt it and licked it all over, and in the joy of reunion let Isa milk her. This went on for some days, and she was so thoroughly deceived that when Isa took the poor stuffed thing, and threw it carelessly aside, the cow went for him for not treating her child with respect ; and so we thought the problem was satisfactorily solved.

But all this happened in very hot weather ; and, as the skin was not cured in any way, it began to smell abominably. So I told them to put it on top of the wood pile to get thoroughly baked with the sun when not in use. Next morning Isa came to me with a very long face. A dog had stolen the wretched calf and it was nowhere to be found, and consequently there was no milk ; and true enough, that cow was no more use and we were compelled to sell her to a butcher.

One of the cows we had was quite a good milker, when suddenly for no apparent reason she went off badly. We could not understand it, and strongly suspected that someone was helping himself ; which made the men very indignant when we suggested it. Late one afternoon we were crossing a field outside our house, where the cow was grazing, and to our utter astonishment saw the old black cow patiently standing with two little girls holding her head rope, while underneath her squatted a small boy with a hunk of bread in one hand, happily having his tea from her in the manner of her calf. Of course, all three bolted when they saw us, but my husband chased and caught the small boy, and gave him the fright of his life. He owned that he had fed himself like this for a long time, and our servants were triumphant that they were inno- cent. That same cow was quite ferocious with strangers and yet she let those children play this trick on her.

One day a Hindu came to me to ask if he might pay his homage to my black and white cow. To the Hindu the cow is a sacred animal, and the man went into some

rigmarole that by feeding my cow he would do some
good to his mother who had lately died. My cow was
chosen because she had a white forehead. Our
Mohammedan servants told me not to let him do any
such thing, as he would cast an evil eye on her and
she would die : but I said it would do her no harm
and he might do it, if it was any comfort to him. So
every morning he came, and after salaaming to the
cow, fed her with a mixture of rice and butter, which
she thoroughly appreciated ; then, when she had
finished her nice breakfast, he wiped her mouth with
an embroidered handkerchief and, bowing low again,
went away.

This went on for several days, till the silly old thing
began to think too much of herself, or else the unusual
food disagreed with her, for sure enough she stopped
giving milk and our servants said : " We told you
so ! " I had to tell the Hindu that he must transfer
his attentions to somebody else's cow ; and after a
while he came back quite happy, as he had found
another suitable animal with a white head, and in a
few days, with careful dieting, our cow recovered.

The meat in Kashgar was very bad, almost too tough
to eat without it being minced ; the mutton often had
a very strong and, what my husband called, a " rammy "
flavour, and the only part of beef it was at all possible
to use was the undercut. In winter we got yâk's
meat, which was much better than the ordinary beef,
also wild duck and game. But it was a difficult job to
make appetising meals.

As the servants were all Mohammedans, I always

cooked anything to do with a pig myself, though we rarely had anything but bacon in that line, for fresh pork they seemed to feel was much more unclean than " bakin," which had come out of a tin and had travelled by post from India. In the winter I used to get some Chinese poik from the New City, and smuggle it into the house and into a big jar of salt, without anyone knowing. After a while it appeared in slices in the kitchen under the name of " bakin " !

Each year, when the frost set in, we killed two or three calves we had brought up and fed well, and some sheep we had fattened for some months, to try and have some good meat during the winter. Though we got a butcher in to do the business, I had to superintend if I wanted the joints properly cut, and also I was forced to keep a sharp watch on the kidneys, and such titbits, or they would disappear, and the men would solemnly declare that that special kind of sheep or calf had no kidneys or liver, as the case might be. But how I hated and dreaded that day's work, for the profession of a butcher has never appealed to me. It was the only way, though, to get palatable things. The next day was almost as bad, when the heads must be prepared and put into salt for brawn, etc., and all the fat cooked for our supply of dripping, on which I depended so much for cooking.

The sheep of Kashgar were of the fat-tailed variety. Their tails were just a solid lump of fat, which often weighed as much as twenty pounds after cooking and clearing, and made fine hard, white, tasteless dripping that could be used for anything.

All our water had to be carried up from the river. We had large wooden pails made for our three horses, and after a few exciting moments when the pails were first put on their backs, they did the work quite happily and often walked into the kitchen while the pails were being emptied, in the hopes that I would be there to reward them with bits of apple or sugar.

The water was the colour of chocolate and as thick when it arrived, and was poured into great earthenware jars. After standing a day, it was transferred into other clean jars for some hours, when what was wanted for drinking was boiled, and poured into a smaller jar to cool and settle again, and by the time it was ready for the table and had been well aerated by pouring it backwards and forwards from one jug to another, it was clear as crystal and quite safe to drink.

Goitre is very bad in Kashgar and worse still in Yarkand, where it is not uncommon to see people with three great swellings hanging one below the other from the throat to the waist. The Chinese never drank any cold water at all but used tea, made with well-boiled water, and none of the Chinese ever seemed to develop goitre, which looks as though the unboiled water had a good deal to do with the cause of the disease. We Europeans, too, who boiled all our water, never had a sign of it.

On certain great days, such as the King's birthday and the New Year, we gave big entertainments to the Chinese Ambans and British subjects. The latter made their own arrangements, and all we had to do was to give them the garden and pay the bills. The Mohammedan part of the community took the lower garden, where they put down carpets under the trees, set up cooking pots and had their feast to the music of a native string quartet. After dinner, we paid them a visit and watched some of the dancing. One of our post runners, a Ladakhi, was an expert dancer, and he was always called upon to give us a very wild Tibetan sword dance, in which he lunged at various spectators with his sword, wearing during the performance the most ferocious expression on his face: this always caused a thrill of excitement.

After sitting awhile among our Mohammedan guests we went to the upper garden to visit the Hindus. The garden was always divided up into several parts with screens of matting, so that the different castes could eat without being seen by people of another caste. They made music on what looked to me like brass pudding basins turned upside down, on which they thrummed with the fingers; evidently the music to them was thrilling, for the singers gazed heavenwards and sang as though they were enraptured, while someone slowly danced, holding a small table cloth stretched out behind his head. And there our guests sat from morning till it was dark. In winter, of course, the entertainment had to be held in a room.

But the dinner to the Chinese Ambans was quite another affair for me. Sometimes if, for any reason, I did not feel up to producing a twelve-course dinner, we gave a real Chinese entertainment, but it was never so much appreciated. In that case, we simply told a Chinese caterer that we wanted a first, or second class dinner, as the case might be, for so many guests, and he knew exactly what to serve. He provided the tables and chairs, bowls, chopsticks, etc., brought his own cooking pots and steamers, for a lot of the Chinese dishes are steamed, and set them up outside the kitchen door. All we had to do was to clear the dining-room of our furniture and pay the bill, which ran up to as much as £30 for a dozen people, served with a dinner that included swallow's nest, or about £20 for one that had sucking-pig for the chief course. Thus a Chinese dinner was a very costly affair, and we rather grudged the money when we found that the guests were disappointed that they were not to have English food.

When I served the dinner, it meant days of preparation beforehand. Cookery books had to be studied, and enough courses arranged to keep our guests busy for three hours at least. To make an impressive start, we began with numerous *hors d'œuvres* and followed with soup. Then I made up all sorts of little fancy things with fish, meat, eggs, poultry, bacon, vegetables, and what was always voted a great delicacy, because they were not sure what the dish was made of—" Angels on horseback." The name pleased the Chinese fancy, and the bit of cheese and haddock (of the tinned variety) rolled up in bacon, and set on a round of fried bread, was very mysterious and dainty. Then I always served several kinds of hot and cold sweets, ending with a big plum pudding that was brought in well alight. That was looked upon as the *pièce de résistance*, and they called it " eating fire." So we went on, sending in one thing after another, until one of the guests sent a message to me that they had had enough, and then I sent in the final coffee, and heaved a sigh of relief that it was all over. They drank their coffee in great haste and hurried away with the polite remark that, put into English, would be : " My stomach is like a drum," the best tribute they could pay to a good dinner.

I had a large box of sweets I had taken out to Kashgar with me for very special occasions. When I was setting the table for our first Chinese dinner, by way of decoration, I put dishes of these sweets down the centre, and I innocently put out all I possessed, thinking that only a few would be eaten, and the remainder I should be able to put back for future entertainments. After the guests had gone I went to collect up my bonbons, but to my dismay found not one left. My husband coming into the dining-room at that moment told me how the Hsie-tai had called his servant, telling him to hold out a large coloured hand-kerchief while he emptied all the bowls of sweets into it, with the injunction to take them home to his children. I was very careful after that never to put out more sweets or biscuits than I meant people to eat.

I mostly went straight to bed after such a feast, utterly worn out and feeling I never would want to see or taste food again. But it was all a part of our job and a very necessary part.

It is comparatively easy to serve up a big dinner from the kitchen, and not have to appear at all ; but when, however, we entertained the Russians officially,

I had to prepare everything first and trust to the men to serve the dinner, because I had to sit at the head of the table and try to appear as though I had not a worry in the world, when all the time my mind was on what dreadful things might be happening in the kitchen.

One day when I was waiting for the joint to appear, a Cingalese boy we had at the time, who spoke English, came running to me and said in a loud stage whisper : " Memsahib, the meat essmelles." I rushed out to the kitchen, and sure enough the meat did smell horribly. It was intensely hot weather, and the heat of the oven had just finished the turning process. What was to be done, for there was a table full of hungry people waiting ? I flew to the store cupboard and got out some tins, which we feverishly opened, heated the contents and put them in a dish with a border of mashed potatoes round, and sent them in. And our guests never knew what a shock to my nervous system I had just had.

The first big plum pudding I made for our Chinese entertainment at the New Year came to a sad end. I left the puddings I had made boiling until evening in Isa's charge, telling him to take them out of the pots and hang them by their strings on nails to drain, when he had finished his work in the kitchen. As we were settling down to a cosy evening after dinner, Isa came in, looking very scared and said : " I don't think the big pudding is quite well, will the Memsahib come and see ? " I rushed out to the kitchen, and there was my beautiful pudding a shapeless mass on the floor. Isa had never thought to see that the knot of the string was firm before hanging it up, and so the poor pudding looked very unwell indeed. I will not enlarge on my feelings, but it was a very real tragedy to me when I knew I could not easily replace the ingredients it had been made of. At that time I had not got enough words to say much, and poor Isa was nearly as upset as I was at the accident. One does not mind these things so much when one can send to a shop and get just what one wants, but it is rather heartbreaking to see stores wasted that one will have to wait months to replace.

After our first Indian cook left, I never found a trained man again, and had to be my own cook practically all the time I was in Kashgar. Later, after Isa's reign, I took a Tibetan, named Lassoo (he who sang sweet music to the cows), and trained him for five years. He was quite intelligent and at last was able to relieve me of most of the work.

On the great day of King George's Coronation, we had to entertain the Chinese, Europeans, British subjects, and a lot of natives—a huge affair. As my youngest boy Robin was only four weeks old, Lassoo had to do all the cooking, and he managed so well that my husband gave him a good bukhshish, and told him he might consider himself a finished cook. A fortnight later he died and I was left stranded again ! We felt his death keenly, for he was a very trustworthy, faithful servant, and we were genuinely attached to him.

At that time I really was rather in despair, for I had a small baby, as well as two bigger children, who, happily, had a good governess to look after their education. Possibly if I had known the difficulties that lay ahead of me, I should not have thought I was so badly off.

We tried many times to get a cook from India, but came to the conclusion that it was better to put up with the inefficient Kashgaris. The only men who would come so far as Kashgar were men who could not get situations in India because of something in their characters that was against them. One or two did come up to us, but they were quite impossible, and they made trouble with the other servants by their intrigues. One man was a good cook, but he swindled us at every turn, and was mostly drunk when it was time to cook our dinner. So I felt that I would rather do the work myself and have peace and quiet in the household.

CHAPTER VIII

OUR FIRST LEAVE, AND RETURN TO KASHGAR WITH AN INCREASED FAMILY

AFTER I had been abroad about four years, my husband applied for long leave, and, feeling sure that it would be granted, I began making arrangements, and building castles in the air of all we would do when we got back to civilization.

It so happened that the Indian Munshi applied for leave about the same time; and when the answer to our application came back, leave was granted to both, but my husband and the Munshi could not be away together, and my husband was left to decide which of them went first. We wanted to go so desperately badly, and I had impulsively told my mother we should be coming home. But, on the other hand, the Munshi had his family in India, and wanted to see them just as much as I wanted to see mine. It was a hard thing to bring ourselves to decide, but the Munshi won, and our leave was postponed for another six months. In June, 1902, Captain (now General) P. J. Miles arrived from India to officiate for my husband, and we joyfully started out from Kashgar with crowds of people to give us a send-off, at " the edge of the carpet " as the saying is, but in this case it was at the edge of the oasis.

As I did the journey backwards and forwards six

times altogether, I will not describe this one in detail, because we went over very much the same ground as we did in coming, with the exception that we crossed the ridge of the Thian-Shan by the Taldik pass instead of the Terek. At midsummer the Terek pass is closed on account of avalanches, and caravans must go by the Taldik, which, for about a month, is free from snow, and has a wide easy road over it ; but it is a considerably longer way.

Except for the flooded rivers, it was a joy to travel in the mountains in summer. On the Russian side, the hills and valleys were carpeted with grass ; and flowers, edelweiss, forget-me-nots, columbines, gentians, violets, veitches, were growing in profusion. Wonderful climbers, such as jasmines, and clematis, and some I did not recognize, hung down in trails from the rocks and overhanging cliffs ; and the birds sang all the time.

It was a time when the Russians in Central Asia were in a specially suspicious mood where Britishers were concerned, for, to our surprise, we found at Irkeshtam, an officer and three Cossacks waiting for us to escort us through Russian Turkestan. We did not much appreciate the attention, but could not say so. We pretended therefore that we were very grateful to the Russian Authorities for being so thoughtful for our safety and comfort. The officer and one Cossack attached themselves to us, and the other two Cossacks joined our servants, and they never let us out of their sight for a moment. We found arrangements made for us wherever we stayed, and everything was quite

comfortable ; but we were simply prisoners, and very
unpleasant it was.   I disliked intensely always having
those men riding close to us, and watching everything I did. We were not allowed to take any photo-
graphs, nor to speak to anyone on the road unless the
officer heard everything that was said.

Our two faithful followers, Jafar Ali and Isa Akhun,
came with us as far as Osh, and were literally in tears
when the moment came to say goodbye, and I was
almost in the same condition. My husband tried to
cheer them up by saying : " Well, anyhow, you are
going to have a very kind Sahib to serve while we are
away." " Yes, maybe," sobbed Jafar Ali," but, you
see, we know the worst of you, but we have yet to find
out the best of him ! "

We started off from Osh on our drive to Andijan
with our officer, or rather " keeper," in a big comfortable carriage with good springs, that he had com-
mandeered for us, but we very nearly ended our lives
in it. When we changed horses halfway, the horse in
the centre shied so badly that he had to be put into
the shafts and harnessed with a sack over his head : I
said I did not like the look of him at all, but everyone
declared that he would be all right when once he got
going. After the first exciting few moments he quieted
down, and went quite steadily, until we came to a
wooden bridge over a flooded river. The planks of
the bridge rattled and frightened him, so that he swung
right round, dragging the other horses with him ;
broke the shaft ; and the carriage was thrown with
such force against the wooden side of the bridge that

it broke away, and the carriage just remained balanced over the broken edge ; while we scrambled out, and the menfolk managed to drag it back. It was a very lonely part of the road, with no houses near ; and if we had gone over into that rushing water, we should simply have been washed away, and no traces left. My husband and I looked at each other speechless, too shaken to do anything, but the fright affected our officer in the opposite way, for he flew at the driver, beat him, and punched him in a mad frenzy, and probably would have killed him if my husband had not interfered. It was not the poor man's fault, for he had to drive the horses that were given him. We finished our drive into Andijan in darkness ; with the shaft tied up with a bit of rope and the horse so unnerved that he shied at everything he met on the road.

When we got into the train, we found that our keeper had spoken to the guard about the " dangerous spies " he had in charge, and a coupé was reserved for us, while he had his seat immediately outside our door in the corridor ; when we went to the dining car he followed ; and if we got out to have a walk on the platform he was close beside to see that we spoke to no one.

The coupé we had was really for ladies only, and next door was one for gentlemen ; but one lady was occupying it. In the middle of the night we stopped at Askabad, a big station, and a crowd of people got on to the train, and evidently one gentleman was without a place. We kept very quiet with our light out to see what would happen ; and we heard the guard come

to our officer and say that he must separate us—put
me with the lady and my husband with the gentleman.
But the officer would not hear of it. He did not know
what mischief we might do if we got with other
people! They argued heatedly for a while and then
the officer whispered something to the guard, evidently telling him who we were and how dangerous
we might be. The guard opened the door of the next
compartment, where the lady was lying *en déshabille*
with her hair in curlpapers, shoved in the extra gentleman, and slammed the door. Then a storm began.
The lady shrieked hysterically, calling the intruder
all sorts of names; the man shouted back, and they
argued till they were tired; and then all became
quiet. Next morning we met them in the dining
car, having breakfast together, evidently in a most
friendly way, and last night's storm was over and
forgotten.

Our officer remained with us until he had seen us
safely on the boat to cross the Caspian Sea; and the
last we saw of him was when he was pointing us out
to a policeman on the quay.

We had intended staying at home for a year, but
were obliged to get an extension of leave, for our
eldest boy, Eric, arrived just as our year was up.

So, in February, 1904, we started off again for our
Central Asian home, with our family doubled; for
having a baby, we must have a nurse, too. He was
only five months old; and it seemed a pretty risky
thing to take such a small traveller on a journey like
the one before us. From the very first we did all we

could to harden him, and accustom him to being out
in all weathers ; and we gave him only cold food. He
throve on the treatment, and never took cold ; and
when we came to travel with him, he stood the journey
better than any of us.

The food question was rather a difficulty ; for we
were afraid of his having milk we were not certain
about, and, on the other hand, we did not want to give
him preserved food entirely for the whole five or six
weeks. We had decided to go by boat from Mar-
seilles to Batoum, as being better for the baby than so
much railway travelling : so we arranged with the
Aylesbury Dairy Company to supply us with enough
bottles of sterilized milk to last us to Batoum ; and
this we had put in the cold storage on the boat. From
Batoum onwards Eric's diet was Allenbury's food,
mixed with well-boiled water, and left to get cold.
When we were in the mountains, his bottles for the
day were prepared before starting the march, and
carefully packed in a bag to be slung over a man's
back. As they needed no heating, he could be fed
when the time came for his meals, and just wherever
we happened to be. And the poor little chap had his
meals in some funny places—cowsheds, in the shelter
of a large rock, or anywhere where we could get out
of the wind. We had the body of his perambulator
carried along with us, in which he slept at night.

Our nurse, Miss Fannie Heath, was a wonderful
woman. She had been in my family since I was a
small child, and was devoted to us all and utterly
unselfish. Although she was not young, nor very

robust, her spirit of determination, and devotion to her charge carried her through all the hardships and difficulties of the road without a grumble.

The same two servants met us again, but we found poor old Jafar Ali very ill, and quite unfit for the return journey through the mountains.

When they came to us at the same dirty hotel in Andijan his greeting to the " Chota (little) Sahib " was pathetic in the extreme. He went up to the bed where the baby was asleep to salaam to him, and with weakness fell down beside him sobbing. Captain Miles had tried to persuade him to let someone else come to fetch us, but he said : " No, I came to Kashgar with the Sahib from India when he first came ; I fetched the Memsahib, and now I must go for the Chota Sahib." There is a wonderful depth of real affection and love in these simple people.

Before we got halfway across the mountains, we had to make arrangements with some Kirghiz to let him stay a day or two with them to rest, and then follow us on slowly. When he reached Kashgar some time after we did, we saw he would never work again, and my husband applied to Government for a pension for him, which was granted. Sad to say he only enjoyed it for a very few months. However, before he died, he had the satisfaction of being appointed Jamadar (head office servant paid by the Indian Government) of the British Consulate after its establishment.

So now life was altogether changed, and I never had to wonder how to fill up my time. It was more often a puzzle how to fit in everything that had to be done, especially when two years later our little daughter Sylvia arrived. Then our hands were full indeed.

All the children's clothes and most of our own we were obliged to make; and, although we had a woman to do the washing, we never could teach one to iron things nicely, and preferred to do it ourselves.

It was so difficult to get articles sent us by post, for parcels were limited to seven pounds weight, and it is surprising how little will go into a parcel so limited, when strong packing must be included. My husband had a pair of thick winter boots sent out once, and they had to come in two parcels, a boot in each !

Parcels from India took about two months to come, and from England nearly three months ; so, from the time we sent our order, we waited four or five months to receive the things ; and when they did come they were often in a terribly battered condition. Even tins arrived bent and twisted. My husband sometimes received cigars from India in the form of powder, which he smoked in his pipe.

One summer I wrote to my mother asking her to send me out a really nice winter hat, as I had nothing' to wear in the cold weather. Months went by and no hat arrived, though I had heard that it was sent off well packed in a strong wooden box, and sewn up in canvas. My mother described it as a beautiful big brown velour hat, trimmed with ostrich feathers, the fashion of that day, and I was looking forward with much pleasure to having it. At last one day a parcel arrived, looking like a big hard sausage firmly sewn up in canvas, and addressed to me in a strange handwriting. When I opened it, never dreaming what I was to find, there was my beautiful hat with feathers and trimmings all rolled up as tight as possible to make a neat package. Evidently the box had come to pieces, and some kind Indian postmaster had repacked the contents, and no doubt was very proud of his neat job.

As I possessed no other winter hat, I had to wear the wreck, because there was no possible way of getting another ; so I ironed and pressed it, and got something to put on my head, but it was neither a beautiful nor a smart creation.

That poor hat was ill-fated, for when I took it out of the box the next winter, after it had been packed away for the summer, out jumped a mouse with a swarm of babies. She had bitten up the feather to make a lovely soft nest in the crown, and had brought up her successive families in it all through the summer. So now my hat had a strong mousy odour, which, in spite of washing and airing, never left it. But again it had to be worn, as it was too late to order another, and probably another would have arrived in the same mutilated condition.

One night a thief got into our storeroom, a half-crazy man, who turned everything upside down ; filled my fur coat with soap and sugar ; and went off with a few things, but, as we thought, nothing of much consequence. He was soon caught by the Chinese and brought for us to see him, chained to a heavy iron bar that he had to carry about with him. When he saw me, he smiled and salaamed, and then took a bundle out of his coat which he presented to me. It was an almost new coat to a winter costume I had hardly worn, all cut up into ribbons. I nearly wept before them all, for the winter was coming on, and I could not replace it.

So life had its trials and worries; which to me, cut off from shops, were not such small ones.

Another worry was to keep our clothes from being eaten up by the moths and their caterpillars; they got into everything made of wool and ate huge pieces out in a very short time, rendering the garments quite unwearable. Moth balls and preservatives utterly failed to keep them away, and I found that the only thing to do was to hang woollen things, furs, carpets, etc., out in the baking sun for a whole day every week or two. That added to the usual work considerably, but when clothing was so difficult to get, we had to take every care of what we had.

It is not very surprising that parcels suffered in the post when one thinks of the road between India and Kashgar. The mail, after the voyage from England, and the railway journey through India to Rawal-pindi, came by cart to Srinagar; from Srinagar through Gilgit and Hunza to Sarikol, it was carried by coolies on foot over the most difficult mountain tracks, too bad for loaded ponies. From Sarikol, our own men fetched it on horseback. We kept four men and horses, for the purpose of taking the post backwards and forwards to and from Sarikol; and they took about a fortnight to do the double journey. It was pretty hard work for them, for it was a difficult road

they had to traverse. In summer they had the flooded
rivers to contend with, and in winter snow, and cold,
and the danger of frostbite.

So, considering the bad roads, and difficulties
between us and India, it always seemed to me rather
wonderful that the mail came as well as it did.

We lost a few posts through the men carrying them
being overwhelmed by avalanches. Sometimes the
men themselves escaped by throwing down their loads
and running for their lives ; but unhappily sometimes
they too were swept away and killed.

The post bags were generally recovered when the
snow melted, and we got our letters and parcels
eventually, soaked with mud, the letters almost
unreadable, and the contents of the parcels often badly
damaged.

Kashgar and the surrounding country stands at
about 4,500 feet above sea level, and the climate is
very healthy, so we were able to keep the children
with us.

We had great extremes of temperature : in winter,
though we had very little snow, the thermometer went
as low as eight degrees below zero Fahrenheit, that is,
forty degrees of frost. But being such a dry cold,
with plenty of sunshine, it was not at all unpleasant.
One had to be careful though, for every winter people
were frozen to death, and it was not uncommon for
travellers to arrive at a caravanserai, with legs frozen
without their knowing it, as the horse plodded
along.

At the beginning of winter, we put up double

windows, and found that we could keep the house quite comfortably warm, by means of the big Russian stoves built into the walls, that reached right up to the ceiling, and in which we burnt wood. These stoves were lit two or three times a day, and the wood allowed to burn until it was reduced to glowing ashes, when the stove was shut down. The whole of the surface then kept quite hot for hours.

We had frost until about the middle of March ; and by the middle of April we were wearing summer muslins. In the autumn, too, the change was just as rapid. April and May were delightfully warm and comfortable. June was hot, and in July and August we often had one hundred degrees Fahrenheit in the rooms. The stones in the courtyard were so hot in the middle of the day that one could not walk across them in thin shoes without painfully feeling the heat through the soles. The nights, too, at that time were so uncomfortable in the house that we pitched tents in the garden and slept outside. Still because the climate was so dry, we were not overpowered by the heat as we should have been in a moist country.

The air was always highly electrical, which made one's hair crackle, and stand on end when combed, and made one's finger nails crack and become brittle.

Only about two inches of rain fell in the whole year, and that generally came in huge thunder deluges that caked and hardened the ground making it necessary to loosen and break up the surface if plants were not to be ruined. Often fields had to be ploughed up and re-sown after a thunderstorm. The farmers depended entirely upon their irrigation canals for watering, and hated the rain.

The ground was wonderfully fertile when cultivated, and produced several crops in a season. Lucerne was raised for purposes of fodder, and it grew quite 4 feet high, being cut four or five times. Strange to say, it formed the first green vegetable we ate in the Spring. Early in March the native children went out into the fields, and dug out the tiny new shoots that had barely appeared above the ground, and sold them by the basin full. Cooked as spinach it was very good indeed.

The length of the summer, and the great heat of the sun made the crops very abundant; and the hotter the weather the more plentiful was the supply of water for irrigation, for the sun melted the ice of the glaciers, and the snow in the high mountains; thus filling the streams and rivers which carried the water down to the plains. A few cloudy days immediately lowered the water in the rivers.

What we most dreaded were the dust storms that came chiefly in the spring and early summer. Let me quote one instance. One day, away across the desert, I saw from my window what looked like a great black pillar advancing towards us through the clear air, with the sun shining on either side of the black mass. It grew bigger and bigger, while the sun became a ball of red before it disappeared entirely. On the other side of the river, the trees were bending, and over us an uncanny stillness hung. The sky grew darker and darker, and then I heard the wind shrieking in the distance and knew from experience that it was time to shut all windows and doors. I had just taken this necessary precaution when with a roar, the storm burst upon us. The trees bent as though they must break and it grew dark as night ; while the dust in the air penetrated through the cracks and crevices covering everything, making it difficult even to breathe. The force of the wind was so great that it was well-nigh impossible to stand against it, and if one was unfortunately caught out on the road or desert in a bad " buran," as these storms were called, the only thing to do was to lie down with the head covered until the first force of the gale had broken. The wind generally lasted about twenty-four hours, and then for days afterwards there was a great calm, though all the time we were in a pea soup fog, not of London smoke, but of falling dust. If at such times a piece of white paper was left lying about, very soon there was a coating of dust on it thick enough to write your name in. Incidentally, I may mention that some people believe that the soil of Turkestan, which is a loess formation, has been made by the deposit of dust from the air. Dr. Sven Hedin, when he was in Kashgar, made some experiments in this connection by leaving out sheets of paper, and he calculated from the amount of dust collected in a given time, how much the surface of the ground would be raised in a century or so. I am no geologist, and I do not pretend to give an opinion as to whether the soil on which I have lived at Kashgar was of sedimentary or of aerial origin, but somehow it strikes me as if there is a lot to be said for the last-named theory.

One summer a pair of eagles built their nest at the top of a high poplar on the terrace in the garden. Though they were rather unfriendly to us, and showed their objection to our walking beneath their nest by swooping down at us, and even brushing our heads with their wings, we let them stay in order that we might watch their habits.

We knew that the baby birds were just hatched, by the parents flying backwards and forwards to the nest with food; when one Sunday morning one of these terrific storms came on. Feeling anxious about them in such an exposed position, we fought our way against the wind to the garden to see how they were faring. There we found the mother-bird sitting on the nest, with her wings outspread, trying to keep the home together and her babies safe, while the tree rocked and swayed in all directions. Her mate flew round wailing and crying, all the time tossed and blown about like a child's balloon. A few hours later, the storm abating, we went again to see how they had fared: there, on the ground, lay the remains of the nest, and six little naked dead bodies, while the bereaved parents were sitting side by side on the terrace wall, crying and moaning like heart-broken human beings. They had done their utmost to save their little ones, but Nature had been too strong for them.

My first Spring in Kashgar came as a revelation to me. The frost that had bound the earth for over five months at last broke, and the thaw set in. At once the branches and twigs of the trees began to take on a lovely green colour, showing that the sap was rising again. The leaf buds quickly swelled in the hot sunshine till one brilliant morning I found to my great joy that, during the night, the buds had burst, and the willows and poplars were hung with catkins that perfumed the air.

Away in the orchard a deep droning sound could be heard, and when I went to investigate I was surprised to find that the garden had turned into fairyland, and was just one mass of lovely pink blossom, while the sound we had heard was from the millions of bees at work among them. The canals were full of water ; and the seeds were whispering to our funny little gardener that they were pushing out as hard as they could go. At night the garden was filled with exquisite music that, at first, puzzled me until I found that it came from swarms of frogs hopping all over the paths. They were fascinating to watch. Mr. Frog hopped along, singing out in a tenor voice : " Diddle-diddle," and from the distance a treble voice answered : " Diddle, diddle, diddle." Away hopped the gentleman in the direction of the voice, and towards him hopped the lady. They met and sat side by side singing a duet in thirds, their throats swelling out like tiny balloons. After they had sung their love duet, away they went together. And so the music went on all night, and every night. Each Spring we listened for the first frog concert, and never lost the thrill of it, for it told us that the long, dull winter was over.

The birds in Kashgar were not very varied.

Sparrows, of course, abounded, and crows, magpies, hawks, kites, rock pigeons, larks, bullfinches, swallows and eagles were common. But the most beautiful were the Golden Orioles and Hoopoes.

The flowers were very poor indeed, and we could get only the hardier English kinds to grow. I think plants from England missed the rain and overhead watering, and probably still more a moist atmosphere.

Trees grew to a great size when planted along the banks of the irrigation canals, and we had fine specimens of willow, elm, walnut, poplars of several varieties, and acacias grown from seed brought from Russia. There was also a tree called by the natives " Jigda "; and I have heard botanists calling it Eligagnus. It had olive green leaves, silvery underneath, and bunches of yellow bell flowers, that gave out a very strong almond scent in spring. The fruit was red and edible, shaped like a small date, with a date-like stone, and very dry, sweet flesh. In the evenings of spring and early summer, the air was heavy with the perfume of the Jigda, and the mignonette-like scent of the grape blossom. Both black and white mulberries grew wild and bore beautiful fruit, intensely sweet and luscious. Our gardener had to climb the trees to pick them, and, finding that the black mulberries stained his white cotton clothes, he had a brilliant idea of how he could save them. I went down the garden one day when he was gathering black mulberries for a pie I was going to make, and discovered the funny little person up the tree stark naked, with his clothes carefully hung on a bush, to be put on when he had finished his job. It did not matter getting himself splashed and stained with fruit juice, his clothes would hide that. So I had to tell him that he must wear his oldest things and spoil them, and I would give him a new shirt and trousers to make up.

But I shall never forget some of the wonderful summer evenings in Kashgar, which began with indescribably lovely sunsets, when the world was just a golden haze that deepened in colour until the sun went down behind the mountains, leaving a sky of orange and red, to fade almost at once into night, fragrant with flowers and filled with the music of the frogs and crickets ; while away in the distance could be heard the singing of the people and the droning of their instruments in the bazaar. It was then that the real spirit of the country was felt, and once experienced, never forgotten.

CHAPTER IX
KASHGARI WOMEN

I soon found that it would be impossible for me to visit much among the native women. There were always so many intrigues going on in their households; and things connected with their family life and love affairs that it was better not to know about. Of course, when a man has several wives, and they all have children, there must necessarily be friction and intrigue, and so the women would come to me, hoping to get me to use my influence with my husband in settling any of their cases that might be connected with British subjects.

I went sometimes to their gala entertainments to see the dancing, and always found it and the company quite fascinating; and I loved to see them in their most elaborate finery, the many vivid colours of the women's and children's costumes making the scene gay and picturesque.

The ladies were very much painted, with eyebrows darkened and made to meet in one long black streak right across the top of the nose; the finger nails on their small neatly-shaped hands were coloured scarlet, and ropes of beads and silver chains dangled round their necks and at the end of their long plaits, making a jingling sound with every movement;

while their black hair literally shone with glue and varnish.

Only the young women like to be slim, and graceful; while the older ones do all they possibly can to grow fat, as a sign of being wealthy and having nothing to do.

I found them self-possessed with graceful manners; and when I arrived at a party, all the guests stood up, and made a low bow, with the hands, covered by the long sleeves, crossed low down, while the hostess greeted me with: "Salaam, Alekhum,"—"Peace be with you, have you come well?" while I tried to bow gracefully in the same attitude, all the time feeling very awkward.

When leaving, the same ceremony was gone through while everyone said "Khosh," meaning "Goodbye."

I sat on a chair, while the ladies sat on their heels on the floor all round the room, with cups, or rather bowls, of tea, sweets, dried fruit, and pistachio nuts before them.

Of course, only ladies were present; and a small orchestra of four or five professional female musicians, who took their turn at dancing, provided the music.

The orchestra was made up of one or two long-necked instruments, with backs rounded like mandolines, played with hair bows and held like 'cellos; other very similar instruments played like mandolines; a zither and a small drum or tambourine. Sometimes for a change the musicians sang. Each spring some-one, I never found out exactly who, composed the new songs that would be fashionable for the year; and one

heard them sung everywhere. The best singers were
the small boys and girls cantering along on donkey
back, singing at the top of their voices to the rhythm
of the donkey's movements.

When the music struck up, one of the professionals
started the dancing and was followed by the guests,
who, one by one, got up and gave a solo dance very
slowly and gracefully, with swaying movements of
the body, and arms, which were held straight out
with the long sleeves hanging over the hands ; the
dancer sometimes simply marking the rhythm of the
music with the feet, while the body remained still with
arms outstretched and eyes closed. The waving and
winding of the arms in perfect time to the music played
a great part in the dance, and was wonderfully graceful
and in keeping with the dreamy music.

With these people, their instruments are merely
sound sources through which they express their
thoughts and feelings, and for that reason they har-
monize so perfectly with the dancing. One could
not help feeling that the music and dancing were
one, both produced by minds cultivated along the
same national lines.

Out of compliment to the dancer, and to show
appreciation of the dancing, the audience in turn got
up, waved some money over the dancer's head, and
dropped it into a receptacle placed before the musicians
and so the more appreciated were the dancers, the
better were the musicians paid.

Many babies and small children were present on
these occasions, and to me they were most attractive.

Little dark-eyed mites dressed in exactly the same way as their parents, in velvet coats and caps and long boots, but they were always shy and frightened of me.

The Kashgari idea of beauty is that the head should be quite flat behind, to make the cap or turban set elegantly, and the long hair hang gracefully; and to achieve this, the new-born babies are tied flat on their backs in their wooden cradles, and are kept lying like that the most of the time till the bones of the back of the head have flattened and no curve or roundness is left.

Both the men and women are devoted to their children, but spoil them utterly. They have no idea whatever of discipline, and give them anything they want one minute and smack them the next.

The babies and small children, go naked in warm weather, and I have often seen some in that costume when I have been very glad to have a warm coat on. They become brown like little niggers, through playing in the hot sunshine.

In time of illness the parents were utterly ignorant and superstitious, and their one idea seemed to be to fly for a witch doctor. I have actually seen children running about the roads in bitterly cold weather, covered with smallpox; then the parents were broken-hearted when children died. Smallpox was a terrible scourge; and the natives would do nothing to keep it from spreading. If it was Allah's will that you or your child took it, nothing could prevent it; and if it was not His will then you would not take it. That was always their attitude about everything and it saved a lot of trouble and worry. They were un-reasoning fatalists.

We, of course, insisted that, if any of the servants had the disease in their homes, they should stay away from us ; but still they would come when they had been in contact with infection, in the hope that we should know nothing about it. However, when they saw that our children did not take smallpox after being vaccinated, some of the men brought their babies, and asked us to vaccinate them.

Nearly all the men and women have venereal diseases, and the children come into the world with that awful inheritance ; and so long as the marriage laws are so slack, it can hardly be otherwise.

The fear of the evil eye is always over the Kashgaris, especially with regard to the children ; and the birth of a baby has all sorts of superstitious practices con-nected with it. It is all kept very quiet and secret and the father is most particular as to who goes near the house or who is the first to touch the child, because of the influence that person will have on the child's nature and destiny. For that reason the missionaries found it very difficult to get the women to allow them to attend them in their confinements ; and they were only called in when the case had gone badly, and it was often too late to do anything to save the mother.

To ensure her confinement being easy, as the time drew near a woman would go and consult a magician, or witch doctor. He made her whirl round and round a pole in the centre of the room, while he chanted some incantations to the accompaniment of a drum beaten by a boy who was his pupil and was studying the art of magic. Round and round she went, till she dropped with giddiness and faintness. If the witch doctor said that all the evil spirits in her were not exorcized, he revived her and repeated the performance until he was satisfied that the cure was complete, when she paid him his fee and went home with her mind at rest that all would go well with her and the child.

This same treatment was used in illness as well, and through it we lost one of our servants, who was ill with pneumonia, for which we were treating him. One day, when we were out, he got his wife to fetch a magician. Happening to pass his house we heard the noise of the drum and the weird chanting, and were horrified to learn that Abdulla was having his evil spirit exorcized. Next day he was dead, and no wonder !

One day we wanted to photograph a particularly attractive little child, and were just getting the camera ready when the mother rushed out and snatched the child away, declaring that the evil eye was in the camera, and if it was turned on to her child it would die.

When I went out first to Kashgar, being a great lover of children, I used to admire the babies, thinking it would please the mothers ; but I soon found that I was very tactless and was drawing attention to the little mite's beauty, which might make Allah want him. If several children in a family died, which was often the case, the parents gave the next baby some very insignificant name, such as " Supurgi," meaning " a broom," " Tash," a " stone," or " Tokhta," meaning " stay," or " stay here," in the hope that Allah would overlook anything so insignificant and humble, and leave it to its parents.

All the children from infancy wore a charm on a cord round the neck to keep them from evil; sometimes it was a verse of the Koran, written on a scrap of paper, and sewn up in leather; sometimes a quaintly carved animal or fish of jade; a stone of some sort; a piece of bone or wood; or just one or two bright beads.

It was a wonder to me that any of the babies lived to grow up, for the custom is that a baby must not be washed for months; and sometimes I have seen tiny mites in an awful state, with sores, skin disease, and ophthalmia in the hot weather. I suppose it is just the case of the survival of the fittest with the mothers and children.

When I first reached Kashgar, after the long journey from England, I wanted a lot of washing done; so my husband told one of the men to find a woman to do it. He fetched one at once, who said she would like the work; but I was surprised when I saw her condition, and horrified when she picked up the heavy bundle of linen and walked off with it to her home. Next day a small boy came to say that his mother was sorry that the washing was not finished, but she had had a baby born in the night. She would bring it to-morrow. And, sure enough, she arrived next day, carrying the finished washing, and the new baby too !

Every week she came and while she did the washing in the back yard, the tiny baby lay on her coat on the ground in a shady corner, and they were both quite well and happy.

One day one of our servants came running to me in great excitement, with what looked to me like a bundle of rags. When I examined it, I found that he had got a tiny baby, which he said he had found. He went to the Mosque to say his prayers, and there on the ground was the bundle. He and his wife were childless and it was a great sorrow and shame to them, and he was sure this baby had been sent from Heaven specially for them. It was a nice little girl about three months old, but oh! so dirty. I suggested a warm bath and some clean clothes that I would supply; and then he could take a nice clean baby to his wife as a present. The men were quite excited and crowded round the happy finder, who would let no one else touch his treasure. He squatted in front of a roaring fire in the servants' room and washed and dressed the infant under my directions, and the little mite kicked about and thoroughly enjoyed the performance. Then we rigged up a feeding bottle, while I gave him a lecture on the right proportions of milk and water; and after the baby had fed ravenously, he triumphantly took her home. A few days after, he came to me very crestfallen, for the child's mother had turned up, as we thought she would, and insisted on having her baby back. In a fit of temper with her husband, she had left his baby in the Mosque to spite him, and would not tell him where it was. Her temper soon

evaporated on thinking of her offspring and she ran
back to get it, to find it had vanished, and she had to
spend some miserable and anxious days hunting for it.
Our man was much upset when my husband told him
that, of course, he must give the child back to its mother.

When a Kashgar marriage is contracted, the Mullah
draws up the divorce paper at the same time, to save
trouble, as it is sure to be wanted sooner or later. A
man then has only to say to his wife before witnesses :
" I divorce you " three times, and the business is done.
So, of course, marriage does not mean a great deal.
Many men marry a girl for the time they are visiting
a place and divorce her when they go away, often after
a day or two, or after some weeks or months, as the
case may be.

A rich old Indian merchant from Yarkand married
a very young and beautiful girl in Kashgar. They
were quite happy together, for he was infatuated with
her and gave her all she wanted. But the time came
when he had to return to Yarkand, and he wanted to
take his wife with him to his old wife and family.
Her father would not hear of it, and said " No " very
firmly, taking her back with him to her old home.
The agreement was that she was his wife in Kashgar,
and nowhere else.

That night the husband got together his friends,
and they stormed the father's house to try and take
the girl by force, making such a disturbance in the
city that the Chinese sent to my husband to ask him
to see that his British subjects did not break the peace
by attacking other people's houses.

My husband called the outraged husband and told him that he must arrange things with the family in an amicable way, and there must be no fighting. He meekly agreed and we thought how reasonable he was. After a while we ourselves went to Yarkand; and on our arrival this same man met us, with the story that the girl had found that she could not live without him, and had come to him in Yarkand; so now everything was all right.

Then we heard the true story, which was this: As soon as my husband had left Kashgar, some friends of the girl went to her father to ask if she might go with them to a wedding in the country. They were dressed in their best and had a sheep tied on behind the cart as a wedding present. The father, never dreaming that these friends were in the pay of the girl's husband, gave his consent and the girl innocently went with them. As soon as they were outside the city, the friends jumped out of the cart, untied the sheep, the driver whipped up the horse, and away the girl was taken to Yarkand, beautifully kidnapped. The father was furious at the trick played on him, and vowed vengeance on his son-in-law, but the girl stayed in Yarkand, whether willingly or by force we never knew.

The women age very quickly, for a girl is married at twelve, and by the time she is twenty-five she looks an old woman, and has probably been married several times and has a large family.

As in all Mohammedan countries, the women do not mix with the men in a social way. They have their own entertainments and they visit each other ; they are not supposed to have any part in religion, and never go to the Mosque for prayer. But there are many shrines, or graves of saints, where they go to wail and pray when they want a child or a husband, or when they are in any trouble or difficulty.

There was a very popular shrine just opposite Chini-Bagh, where we could hear the women wailing from early morning. It was the grave of a female saint called Anna Bibi, but what she had done in her life-time to have the power to help those who called upon her, I do not know. The women who were looking for husbands knelt before the tomb, putting their hands into two holes while they cried and wailed by the hour. I sometimes suspected that their prayers were answered pretty quickly, for I often saw youths wandering about near the shrine, furtively inspecting the supplicants.

Another shrine used to be stuck all over with dabs of mud. There the people went when they wanted to be cured of some skin disease. They took lumps of mud from a well near by and threw them against the wall of the shrine, at the same time praying to the saint.

In all probability these saints had been just half mad beggars in their lifetime. There were many such people, both men and women, and even whole families wandering about the old graveyards, and living in the old tombs, and shrines. They were looked upon by the people as being especially holy, and were never refused food and money.

We had rather a startling experience with one of these poor creatures. One New Year's morning we had just finished breakfast, and my husband was lighting his pipe in the hall. For warmth during the very cold weather, we kept the front door locked and bolted, using a door at the end of the hall. I was just remarking " I wonder who will be our ' firstfoot ' this year," when we heard footsteps on the verandah, and next moment the front door was wrenched open with tremendous force, that broke the lock and bolts right off. In rushed a wild, fantastic looking beggar, who threw himself full length at my husband's feet sobbing and crying that " They were after him to kill him."

Our servants hearing the noise came running in, and got hold of the man, putting him on his feet. Then my husband tried to get some coherent story from him, but all he could say was that " They wanted to kill him." Suddenly he broke away from the men, who were holding him, and dashed off towards the city at such a speed that he was lost sight of.

Next day he was found in an old tomb in one of the graveyards dying. He had literally almost cut himself to pieces in the mad frenzy that was beginning to take possession of him when he broke into our house.

I suppose the demoniacs who were possessed of devils in Bible times were just these same poor epileptics.

And our tragic visitor was our " firstfoot " for that year !

Another strange story comes to my mind of a poor old woman we rescued one Christmas Eve. Quite

near our home was a big Chinese Cemetery. A
wizened old Chinaman was in charge of it, and lived
in a room built beside the gate with a wretched looking
native woman.

One morning I was passing by, and saw a coffin
being carried out of the old man's room, while the
woman was sitting on the ground some distance away
looking rather strange; but, as there were some
Chinese nearby, I did not speak to her. Next day our
children said they had seen her still sitting in the same
place; and two days after, they came home from a
drive with the story that she was sitting in the same
position on a dunghill outside the City wall; and she
looked as if she was frozen stiff, though she did not
seem to be dead. It was bitterly cold and snow had
fallen, and no human being could survive being out
all night. So after tea my husband and I took a
lantern, and set out to see if we could find the poor
creature. It was very dark, but at last we discovered
her sitting on a manure heap motionless. I spoke to
her, but could get no reply, beyond a movement of
her eyes when I offered her some bread.

I opened her coat, and to my surprise found food
and money on her lap that passers-by had given her,
but which she could not eat, or even hold, for she was
frozen perfectly stiff: only her brain seemed to be
alive. If she had not had the warmth of the unsavoury
heap she was sitting on she would have died long
before.

Some men with donkeys came along, and we asked
them if they knew who she was, and what had hap-

pened to her. They replied that she was the old woman the Chinese had sat on a fire for punishment because she had tried to burn the old man she had lived with, by setting light to his coffin. Then they had thrown her out to die because she was old, and ugly now, and no one would want her. They seemed to look upon the whole affair as a good joke, and stared at my husband in surprise when he told them to carry her on a donkey to our house. They simply refused and rode away.

So we went home, and told two of our men to get something for a stretcher, and go and fetch her in. They made excuses, and did not want to go, until my husband lost his temper, and told them that they were queer Mussulmans if they would not do a good deed.

Our prison was empty at the time, so we made a fire in one of the rooms, and a warm soft bed of straw in one corner, but when the poor old thing was brought in we found that she was as stiff as stone, and it was impossible to lay her down. So she had to be left sitting in the same position, and we quite thought she must die during the night.

Next day we got her to drink some warm soup, and the day after she demanded some meat. Soon her limbs began to be flexible, and at last she was able to lie down. Then we discovered how terribly she was burnt.

Slowly she recovered, and the burns healed, and then the question was what to do with her. She was very grateful to us, and naturally did not want to leave us, and the comfortable warm quarters she had found.

Although she was living in our prison, I do not suppose she had ever been so comfortable or so well fed, in her life ; and it seemed such a marvel that any human being could live through such treatment.

She was one of the lowest of characters, and not a woman I could have as a servant, so as the Chinese had poor houses of a sort, my husband asked an Amban to arrange for her to have a room in one of these places.

He promised to do so, saying that no doubt we thought we were doing a noble thing to nurse her back to life, when really we should have done much better if we had not interfered, and she had been left to die. She was old and useless, and probably we had just saved her for a worse fate. And I have sometimes wondered if he was not right after all.

CHAPTER X

A SUMMER HOLIDAY AMONG THE KIRGHIZ

BEFORE I had any family I used to travel about with my husband when he went on his tours, and we enjoyed the change after the rather monotonous existence in Kashgar : but when our family increased, we found it such an undertaking to move about, that I remained alone in Kashgar with the children, where, at any rate, we had every comfort possible for them. But the longing for a change of surroundings was great at times. So one summer, when the heat was especially trying, we decided to hunt for a hill station. After many inquiries, we heard of a pretty little valley called Bostan Terek, where there was good water and grass, and also some houses, or rather huts, up in the mountains, some three days' march from Kashgar towards the Pamirs ; and we decided to try a holiday camping among the Kirghiz.

Mr. and Mrs. Högberg, who had left their children in Sweden, agreed to join us ; and after much preparation and many arrangements, we were ready to start.

Everything was packed up overnight to enable us to start early, and so get the march over before the great heat of the day. We had little sleep that night, on account of the stifling heat ; and when we got up at 4 a.m., we found that it was very dull, with thunder in the air.

We had hired eight huge Chinese carts, each drawn by four horses—one in the shafts and three in front; and they were standing ready loaded in the courtyard. But in spite of our efforts to be on the road in good time, we were delayed until past eight, when already the heat was becoming intolerable. The drivers quarrelled about the loading of the carts, each man, of course, wanting to take as little as he could. They shouted and gesticulated, and simply wasted time, until Jafar Bai (Jafar Ali's successor) took matters into his own hands and got things settled; and at last the carts began to move out of the gate. Our nurse and I took the two children, Eric, aged three years, and Sylvia, six months, in our little Russian carriage. Mrs. Högberg went in a small Chinese *marpa* cart, while the gentleman of the party rode. Also, in our train, were both the Indian and Chinese Munshis with their servants. We looked like a caravan of gipsies, with the carts decorated with pots and pans, brushes, and brooms, etc.

Very soon after starting, a terrific thunderstorm came on, and the rain poured down in a perfect deluge, making the road so slippery that the horses had difficulty to keep their feet. There was no shelter anywhere near, so we had to push on, though we were becoming soaked through. We bundled the children up in coats and rugs, and cuddled them close to us, and happily they slept. Just as the storm was abating, we reached a little village where we got shelter in a caravanserai. We all crowded into a dirty little room and a kind woman brought us hot tea. It tasted like chopped hay, but it was given us with a smile of welcome. It is remarkable how cosy such a miserably dirty little place can be when one is wet and cold, just because it is dry and weathertight; and how a cup of tea that at any other time we should have thought undrinkable is cheering because it is given with a smile of friendliness.

The storm soon passed, and we started off once more, driving on through country lanes, until we came to the edge of the oasis of which Kashgar is the centre; and we found quarters prepared for us by a rich *mullah* in his fine house. The Kashgaris really are most hospitable, and will put themselves to any inconvenience for European travellers.

Our host received us in the outer courtyard and took us to his *mehman-Khana*, or guest room. It was like a large pillared hall, with a passage through the centre; each side of the passage being a raised platform covered with beautiful native carpets, on which were placed bolsters and pillows for the comfort of guests; and at once light refreshments were placed before us to keep us going till dinner time. We ladies and the children occupied this palatial room, while the gentlemen slept in an inner apartment.

As is usual in a native house, there was only a large skylight for light and air, which in the night let in a downpour of rain when the thunderstorm returned; but we slept very peacefully, for the house was clean and comparatively free from the unwelcome visitors

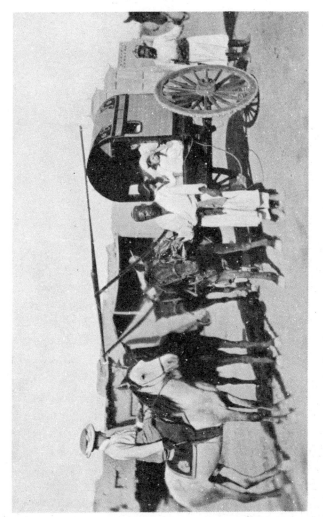

A CHINESE TRAVELLING CART.

that infest most native houses. On a previous journey some years before, my husband and I had put up in another house in the same village, and without any exaggeration, we could not sleep for the noise made by the fleas. They were there in their thousands, hopping and making a popping noise all round and all over us. The soft dry soil is a breeding place for them, and the greatest care is necessary to keep a house in a habitable condition. We even used to get them on us while walking round our own garden. The only remedy was to put Keating's powder everywhere and in everything.

While I am writing of these unpleasant creatures, an old lady comes to my mind who, on hearing of the sort of travelling we were going to do to get to Kashgar, exclaimed : " But, my dear, just think of the fleas ! " To which my husband very quietly replied : " What sort of a British Empire should we have if all Britishers had thought of the fleas ? "

Next morning we started off across another strip of desert, which we reached at lunch time and where we were met by a crowd of people, with refreshments set out under a big shady tree; and an invitation from the Kazi-Kalan, or Chief Mohammedan Magistrate of Opal, to be his guests, when we reached that village. We could not stay the night there, as we wanted to get on further to shorten the march for the next day, but we said we would visit him with much pleasure; and we found him living in a big house with a beautiful garden. The house was native in style, but with the improvement of glass windows.

The Kazi himself was a splendid specimen of a refined, educated Mohammedan gentleman, tall and slim, with thin handsome features and a long, white beard. His spotless turban was beautifully wound, and he carried himself with much dignity. He came out to meet us at his gateway and in the most gracious manner possible took us into his *mehman-Khana*, where he himself set refreshments before us. It is the custom for the host to serve his guests himself, and we could not but feel honoured by being waited on by such a host.

As we had to wait several hours for our tents to be pitched further on, we put the babies to bed and had a good rest ourselves in his cool verandah, while our host and my husband had a long talk.

Before leaving, the Kazi insisted on giving us dinner, which we gladly accepted. I wanted to see what a good native dinner would be like served in such a refined house. We had bowls of soup, curry, and a huge dish of pillau, that is, fried chicken mixed with rice cooked in fat, and in amongst the rice we discovered sultanas, prunes, dates, and pistachio nuts. It was really a delicious dish, for it was made with good fresh fat. I had had pillau made with rancid fat that was too awful for words. Three kinds of native bread were served. Little round cakes about the size of a bun, with a hole in the centre, great flat rounds, about fifteen inches across, rolled out very thin and baked crisp. Both these varieties were made of wheat flour, with a good deal of the bran left in, and sometimes finely shredded onion and linseeds were sprinkled over the thin, crisp bread, which was not at all bad. The third kind was made from Indian corn, and was quite nice when newly baked, though it had rather a bitter taste. This was the bread mostly eaten by the poorer people, and it was certainly very satisfying and solid.

Tea and this corn bread form the staple diet of the common people, and they seemed well able to do long marches, or a hard day's work, on it.

We all sat tailor fashion on the floor and thoroughly enjoyed the good dinner provided for us, in spite of the fact that we had no knives, forks, or plates, and just helped ourselves from the common dish with our fingers in the native way.

That night we camped in tents by the river side, and felt that the holiday we had so looked forward to had really begun.

But the next day's march in a cold white mist, all the time bumping over huge stones, made our spirits begin to droop. It got colder and colder, no mountains were anywhere visible, nothing but this heavy mist that just seemed to suffocate one.

At lunch time, we found some very wild looking Kirghiz waiting by the road side, with a huge black cauldron boiling away over a fire of sticks, and in it a sheep stewing for our luncheon. We stopped when they greeted us, and had to accept from them bowls of soup, with great lumps of fat mutton in it; boiled without a vestige of salt, and which we were obliged to fish out of the soup with our fingers and eat, pretending to enjoy them. Boiled mutton had always been an abomination to me ever since my childhood days ; but boiled mutton minus salt, and served and eaten in Kirghiz fashion, was beyond the limit. But these people had taken the trouble to come over ten miles with it, and the least we could do was to put our feelings aside, and appear to appreciate their kind thoughtfulness.

When, late in the afternoon, we reached the end of the Bostan Terek Valley to find tents pitched for us in the longest, wettest grass, and still nothing but mist to be seen, we sat wrapped up in shawls and blankets, secretly longing for the heat of the plains and our comfortable dry homes, but still insisting to each other that it was great fun.

Next morning things were no better when we got up, and we sat down to breakfast a very silent and subdued company.

Suddenly the sun broke through the clouds ; the mist rolled away like a curtain ; and there, all around were the glorious mountains, with our camping ground just a mile or so up the green valley basking in the sunshine.

How our spirits rose, and we all began to talk and laugh ; even the horses and donkeys tethered outside the tents joined in the chorus of rejoicing !

We hurriedly got our things packed up and off we started ; some of us walking the short distance, and some riding. Up we went along a narrow winding path, through fields of clover and wheat, planted beside a swift running mountain stream, while invisible larks made exquisite music above us. Then across a little bridge to the camp prepared for us.

Bostan Terek is the winter encampment of a colony of Kirghiz. They find it too hot to remain there in summer, and emigrate with their flocks and herds to pastures higher up, leaving their mud huts empty. As they grow their winter supply of wheat and fodder there, a few of the men come down every day from summer grazing ground to work in the fields.

But, although the Kirghiz think the heat in the valley too great, we found it simply delicious and quite cool enough for camp life. It must be over 7,000 feet above sea level; more than 3,000 feet higher than Kasghar.

It was among these primitive habitations that we found a fairly comfortable room that would do as a nursery; with a little mosque beside it. We pitched a large tent for our bedroom, and made some Kirghiz tents we found ready for our use into the kitchen, servants' rooms, etc.; while Mr. and Mrs. Högberg were accommodated in a tiny house consisting of one room and a hall, about five minutes' walk across the valley. We at once set to and thoroughly cleaned out the rooms, making sure there were no scorpions in any of the corners; and then unpacked and made ourselves as comfortable as possible with carpets and camp furniture.

But our tent bedroom, after the first night, turned out to be so airy, not to say cold and draughty, that the next day we nailed heavy Kirghiz felts across the front of the mosque, having first ascertained that the Kirghiz would have no objection, and made that into our room. In spite of the novel sleeping place, or perhaps because of the sanctity of the spot, we passed most peaceful nights of slumber there.

The Kirghiz, though probably we were the first Europeans they had seen, were very friendly and ready to help. They sold us sheep from their flocks, and brought us various kinds of game they had hunted with falcons. Beautiful little red-legged partridges called Kek-liks, that ran all over the hill sides, hares, ulla (a large bird like the Scotch capercailzie), ibex, *ovis Poli*, yâk, and gazelle, all made a welcome change from the eternal mutton and scraggy chickens, of which we got so tired in Kashgar : and once a week we sent a man to Opal to buy eggs, flour, rice, potatoes, vegetables, etc.

Of course, we womenfolk were a great curiosity to the Kirghiz, for they had never seen such strange creatures before. Possibly that summer is still remembered as the time when the "Feranghis" came to live in the valley !

It would be difficult to find a better example of the influence of geographical environment on the conditions of human life than that furnished by the nomadism of the Kirghiz. Their life is essentially a simple one. They have no need of foreign products ; in fact, their flocks and herds supply everything necessary for food, clothing, and even for their dwellings, with the exception of wood, which they find in the mountains.

They dress in sheepskins ; their tents, or Ak-ois, are covered with thick felt made from the wool of their animals ; the wooden lattice framework of the tents is tied together with strips of raw hide ; the ropes used to bind the felts are home-made and of wool ; and even the fuel they use for cooking and heating is the dung from the animals.

Their food consists chiefly of mutton, cooked in different ways. The sheep are of the fat tailed variety, and have tails reaching nearly to the ground, composed of a solid lump of fat.

The milk and cream the Kirghiz use fresh, and also in the form of little sour cheeses or curds, made by allowing the milk to stand till it coagulates. Kumiss, that is, mare's milk, put into a kid's skin and allowed to ferment, is a favourite drink. It is quite nice and refreshing when one is on the march, but decidedly heady. The kid's skin makes a great bottle when the legs are tied up and the neck used as the neck of the bottle.

A man's wealth is reckoned, not by the amount of money he has, but by the number of animals he possesses ; and he uses them as he would use money, for purchasing. Every man buys his wife with cattle, a poor man paying five or ten sheep for his, while a rich one pays for his in horses and camels, according to her age and beauty. The woman also is expected to bring a dowry with her in the form of animals and jewellery.

The Kirghiz have broad flat faces, with high cheek bones and almond eyes, showing that they are descended from the Mongols. The men have little or no hair on the face, and both they and the women have extraordinarily bright-coloured complexions and hard weather-beaten skin, due to their outdoor life and exposure to the elements.

The women, although they are Mohammedans, are very free and go about unveiled. Their dress is much like the dress of the ordinary woman of the plains. But their headdress is a marvellous arrangement of white muslin, wound round and round many times till it looks like an enormous cocoon. Sometimes it is pure white, with silver ornaments and fringed embroidery hanging down over the ears and shoulders, and sometimes the muslin is of a pale colour, with an embroidered edge. The shape and colour of the cocoon varies according to the tribe of Kirghiz.

For full dress, or when they travel to a new encampment, the women put on all their finery and are loaded with necklaces of coral and silver, heavy silver ornaments finish their plaits of hair, and silver rings cover their fingers.

Of course, living this outdoor life makes it impossible for them to be secluded and consequently they are independent and self-possessed.

The men are often away looking after the animals, which wander great distances up the hillsides, or are working in the fields ; and the whole encampment is left to the womenfolk, who do all the work at home of milking, rearing the young animals, bringing up their children, and making the family's clothes. It is also their work to put up and take down the Ak-ois, when they move, and the men stand by and watch them do it. They make also the felts and all the embroideries, and fancy cords and straps for the adornment of their tents.

They do not seem to have large families generally speaking, and the infant mortality is very high, due to the hard winters in the mountains and the pre-vailing ignorance of sick nursing : so the strongest survive and grow up into very hardy men and women.

The women are almost as much at home on horse-back and camelback as the men, and we used to see them riding over the roughest and steepest of roads, carrying a baby and with one or two children riding behind. Certainly the horses were wonderfully sure-footed, and almost like gazelles for climbing over boulders or going down steep paths cut like staircases, and even on ice they kept their feet very cleverly. I have often gone over places on horseback that I could not cross on foot, just trusting to the horse to pick out his own way, instead of hampering him by trying to guide him. This, I suppose, is another instance of the effect of environment and upbringing. But it does puzzle me how horses in civilized countries should have such difficulty in keeping their feet on the tarred motor roads.

All the bowls and utensils for household purposes, with the exception of the iron cauldrons and the copper vase-shaped kettles that are put right down into the heart of the fire to boil water for tea, are made of wood for ordinary use. But for visitors some china bowls are kept carefully packed away in round wooden boxes, made exactly to fit each bowl.

We were highly amused one day to see a baby being

fed from a Kirghiz feeding bottle. It was a tiny kid's skin, filled with goat's milk. The neck was in the baby's mouth, and the mother—or more probably some relative, for it was most likely that the baby was motherless—was squeezing drops of milk down its throat.

The Ak-ois are made by putting up a circle of trellis work first. Upon it are fastened a number of slightly curved poles, fixed into a circle of wood at the top of the tent, which forms the skylight and the opening through which the smoke from the fire immediately beneath it can escape. This framework is covered with thick felts, securely fastened with ropes, and over the skylight a piece of felt is drawn at night. On one side is a doorway closed by a felt curtain ; and the whole structure is generally weighted down with heavy stones to keep it from blowing away in a sudden whirlwind that may come unexpectedly sweeping down the mountain valleys.

We were, on one of our journeys, having dinner in a Kirghiz tent, when suddenly all the felts were lifted up and blown away, and we were left with only the framework round us. Another time a tent that had been carelessly put up collapsed in a gale in the middle of the night, and the occupant was discovered smothered by her dwelling, with her head sticking through the skylight.

When one enters an Ak-oi, one finds on the ground in the centre the fire. On the left side of it are carpets to sit on and piles of bright-coloured padded quilts and bolsters for the family's use at night, and perhaps some fancy boxes in which the household treasures are locked up, the keys of which are kept by the wife on the end of one of her long plaits of hair. On the right-hand side of the tent is a screen of matting worked with bright-coloured wools, and behind this the food and cooking utensils are kept. This is the larder or pantry of the house.

The Ak-ois we found varied in size, some being fifteen feet in diameter, others smaller. They were exceedingly comfortable and spacious to live in, for one could stand upright in any part, except just close to the side where the curved poles joined the trellis, and the points of the trellis made pegs to hang one's things on.

At the end of our stay we invited all the Kirghiz belonging to the valley of Bostan Terek to a dinner. The men accepted with alacrity, but said the women could not come, as they had to stay at home to mind the camp and keep the wolves away from the flocks !

So the day before we started for home, one hundred and ten men and boys arrived in the early morning to prepare the feast. They rode down on various animals—horses, camels, yaks, and even bulls—and these animals were put to graze all over the valley and kept up a chorus of neighing and lowing while the camels screamed in their very original way.

We bought five sheep from the Kirghiz and sent to Opal for a sack of rice, a sack of carrots, another of bread, and two huge baskets of apricots. Our guests cooked the dinner themselves in several enormous iron pots, over fires made between big stones on which the pots rested. It consisted of soup, pillau, apricots, bread and tea. And how they did eat ! I have never seen anyone devour their food as they did. They tore the meat to pieces with their hands, and if they felt unusually friendly to the man they were next to, they poked a special titbit into his mouth. When everything was eaten, they still walked about gnawing at the bones, so that not a bit of goodness should be left to be thrown away.

To assist digestion, after dinner they offered to play a game of " Bargai " for our entertainment. This is their great sport, and it is played on horseback with a dead kid or calf. One man has the animal across his knees, and he gallops away with it, to throw it in some inaccessible place. The other players gallop after him and, still mounted, fight and struggle to get the kid. The winner then goes off with it, after having received a bit of coloured rag which he ties in his belt to show that he has won one round, and throws it down in another place, to be fought for again. When the scrum begins, all the players hold their whips, and sometimes reins, with their teeth, to set the hands free. We sat up on the flat roof of a little house, to be out of harm's way, and to be able to watch the game as it was played around us. It was very exciting and full of thrills, and one wondered how any of the men or horses came out alive. There were a few casualties, and Mr. Högberg had to render first aid, but they were surprisingly few. The horses, too, entered into the spirit of the game and seemed to understand exactly what to do.

The next day was bright and sunny—cool, and lovely in the mountains, but burning hot on the plains, and, as we slowly marched down, getting hotter and hotter, we looked round many times to the little green valley, shining like an emerald between the steep bare rocks of the mountains; but which was growing smaller, and smaller until we could see it no longer; and only the memory of a very happy holiday among the Kirghiz was left us.

CHAPTER XI

A JOURNEY HOME VIÂ NARYN AND CHIMKENT

IN 1908, we, that is to say, my husband, Eric, and Sylvia (then aged five years and two and a half respectively), our nurse, and I travelled home by a route quite new to us, to escape five or six difficult crossings of the flooded rivers that we should have in going to Osh. In crossing the mountains in a northerly direction to Naryn, we should only have to ford the river once.

As this route is little known and intensely interesting, I think I cannot do better than describe it in the form of a diary I wrote at the time. It may be of use or interest to someone thinking of doing the same journey.

At the end of June, 1908, as Captain Shuttleworth rather unexpectedly arrived to take over charge for my husband, we decided to start for home, in spite of the difficulty of travelling during the heat of July. As the usual route viâ Osh was impossible on account of the amount of water in the rivers, we took the road viâ Naryn, and travelled through the province of Semiretchia by tarantass, joining the Orenburg railway at Aris, a little to the north of Tashkent.

After a most strenuous week of packing and preparation, we started, thoroughly tired out with hard work and excitement. Crowds of people gave us a send-off, and, as it was possible to drive for the first three marches, we took our little Russian carriage for Nurse and Eric. One of our Swedish friends, Mr. Anderson, came with us, driving Sylvia and me in his comfortable spring cart ; and so we got over the first part of the road in the heat of the plains with comparative comfort and as little fatigue as possible.

Friday, July 3rd.—This morning we said goodbye to Mr. Anderson and to our carriages, and saw them start on their way back to Kashgar. Then we mounted our ponies, Eric riding in front of Isa on a long pack saddle, and Sylvia in front of John, our Cingalese servant. Our road led up a long, very barren valley, taking us deeper and deeper into the mountains. After seven hours' steady marching, we reached our camping ground, and found Kirghiz tents ready for us ; but we were so stiff and tired with being so long in the saddle for the first march, that we dismounted with difficulty and had to stand for a while before we could walk into the tent. " Aghachi-Kol " (meaning " the woman's hand ") is the strange name of this place, and we have come twenty-four miles to-day, and fifty-nine miles from Kashgar.

Saturday, July 4th.—To-day the weather has been simply perfect for crossing the Karatecki Pass. We have not seen a cloud in the sky, and there has been just enough breeze to make the heat of the sun bearable. There is no doubt about this pass being a difficult one. On the south side we thought it very steep, and from the distance the road looked like some scratches on the side of a gigantic cliff; but, although the road was only a few feet wide, it was of gravel, and the ponies had a good hold for their feet. However, when after an awful climb, we reached the top and looked down the other side, we found that we had something worse before us. There seemed to be no road at all over the great black jagged rocks. The view from the summit quite repaid us for our efforts, and we stood gazing almost with awe at the enormous stretches of mountain ranges all around us. The colouring was so wonderful, for some of the mountains were deep violet and purple, shading to black, others, composed of sandstone, were glowing with shades of red, which made a lovely contrast to the giant peaks white with eternal snow. And those in the far distance were veiled by a delicate grey mist, which made them both ethereal and mysterious.

Somehow the loaded ponies managed to pick their way down among the boulders; and when they were well ahead the men tied our riding animals together in a long string, fastening the tail of one to the bridle of the one behind, and a Kirghiz led them down.

The next business was to get the children down safely; so we put them into two sacks I had made for them for warmth when travelling, out of old padded quilts, and the servants took them on their backs. They looked so funny, with just their heads peeping out, and thought it was a great joke.

Then we followed the procession and our mode of

locomotion could hardly be called walking; it was slipping and sliding the whole time, and that not always on our feet! When we reached the bottom, we looked back, and wondered how we had all managed to get down without any accident; and still more how loaded ponies could · oss such a pass. As soon as the road was comparatively easy, we remounted and after about an hour's ride we suddenly came on the Chakmak River and were joyfully surprised to see on the opposite bank, three Ak-ois waiting for us. The river was shallow and we were soon across it, and found that our camp had been prepared in a lovely meadow full of wild flowers, and even the tents were carpeted with grass and yellow kingcups. This place is called Chakmak, and the distance we have come is fifteen and a half miles.

Sunday, July 5th.—To-day's march has been long and trying. The heat, when we were sheltered from the wind, was almost overpowering. The road was easy enough, and for some hours we kept beside the Chakmak River, which had to be continually crossed and re-crossed. At last we left the river and went round a funny red mountain with a black peak to it, named by the Kirghiz "The Black Hat." After crossing a little pass, we entered a wide valley that looked just like a great plain, with some little ridges of hills poking up here and there. In reality we were right on the top of the Thian-Shan mountains, with only these ridges or peaks above us.

Our guide said that our camp was just round the corner behind one of these peaks, but we never seemed

to get any nearer to it. On and on we wandered,
getting more and more tired and silent, until at last
no one spoke a word. Oh, it was wearisome! There
was a Kirghiz riding in front of me, and every time
he disappeared into a little hollow I cheered up,
thinking he must have stopped at our destination, but
again he appeared riding steadily on, until I began to
feel furious with the poor harmless fellow for dis-
appointing me so often. But all journeys come to an
end; and suddenly from the top of a bit of rising
ground we espied two tents pitched in a little hollow.
My pony, generally a most undemonstrative animal,
gave a happy whinny and set off full trot, he and I
forgetting our fatigue in the joy of seeing so near the
end of one more day's journey. This place has a queer
name, *i.e.*, Tion-debba, so called from a peak on the
summit of which is the grave of a Kirghiz saint.
Twenty-three miles we have done to-day.

But what a desolate wind-swept plain this is, and
the altitude makes us feel sick and queer, and unfit
for any exertion. When the sun went down, the wind
became bitterly cold in spite of this being the month
of July; and to make it a little more comfortable for
the children, we pitched our own little tent inside a
large Kirghiz ak-oi, and put them to sleep in the inner
tent, while we slept on the ground in the little space
between the two.

Monday, July 6th.—This morning we wended our
way up the valley till we came to the tent of the
Russian picket, at the foot of the Turgat Pass. This
official, a Russian Kirghiz, was very civil, and gave us

refreshments; and after a short rest we proceeded to
ascend the pass. The Russians have made a good
zigzag road over the pass, so it was quite easy-going.
On the top there is a pile of stones to mark the frontier
between Chinese and Russian Turkestan, and there we
bade farewell to Chinese territory and crossed over
the border into Russia. And at the same time we had
crossed by the Turgat Pass the crest of the Thian-
Shan. On one side of it, the waters flow eastwards to
Lob Nor, and on the other are the sources of the
mighty river known as the Jaxartes or Syrdaria, which
runs right across Russian Turkestan and empties itself
in the Aral Sea.

After we had ridden down and down for about three
and a half miles, a valley suddenly opened up on our
left, and there in the distance was the Chadir Kul Lake,
looking so blue and peaceful, as it lay at the foot of the
snow-covered mountains. Here we found our camp
ready for us in a little sheltered nook beside a stream.
The whole of the march since crossing the Turgat
Pass has been through lovely undulating meadows,
which are riddled with marmot holes that make rather
dangerous traps for the ponies' unwary feet. The
funny little brown animals, about the size of large
rabbits, were all over the place playing and scampering
about, calling to each other with their peculiar
whistling call. They were most fascinating creatures,
especially the fat little brown babies, which were
scrambling and tumbling over their mothers so
happily until our footsteps were heard. Then there
was a general rush for their respective holes, and the

poor mothers were worried to death until they had got their troublesome families safely underground. Some of the old grandfathers of the tribe refused to show fear, and sat bolt upright above their holes, looking exactly like bits of brown rock until we got quite near. Then down they went and disappeared like jacks-in-the-box.

To-day we are feeling the mountain-sickness badly. That is to say, the adults of the party. As for the children, they are more lively than ever. As soon as we get into camp, they start pillow fights with the cushions put for our use, and their favourite game now is pretending that they are marmots in their holes !

Our Kirghiz host brought us a tray of sugar and sweets, and a pot of Russian raspberry jam, and we were all as delighted as a lot of schoolboys with the jam. To-day the march was only thirteen miles, and we are encamped at the foot of the Turgat Pass on the Russian side.

Tuesday, July 7th.—The most of to-day's march has been beside the Chadir Kul Lake. It was very cloudy and bitterly cold when we got up at five, and while we were having breakfast some hail fell; but, as the day wore on, the weather improved till at last it was bright and breezy. The lake is long and narrow and looks very desolate, lying at the foot of the mountain, with no sign of any sort of life. The intensely blue stretch of water, backed by the purple hills with their white crests, the emerald green plain reaching to the water's edge, and above all the great masses of white billowy clouds sailing along majestically before the wind—all made a beautiful picture, but one that lacked life.   The utter loneliness of the place depressed me. There is a legendary monster or dragon supposed to live in the waters of the lake, who comes out to challenge passers-by, but we saw nothing of him.

As we drew near our halting place, numbers of Kirghiz rode out to welcome us, and to escort us to the tents prepared in our honour.

The Kirghiz of these parts must be very wealthy, for their tents are large and handsomely furnished with rich silk hangings to keep out the draught, padded quilts, and great soft bolster-shaped pillows, all covered with rich bright-coloured silk.   But unfortunately their riches do not seem to make them clean and particular in their habits; for the tents are inhabited by most undesirable companions, that give the poor children a worrying time.   These pests are of a very minute variety, that get right into the wool of one's clothing.   We had great difficulty to find and get free from them; for even washing the garments does not seem to destroy the horrid things.

Our host, a great fat Beg, brought us a Russian samovar and good Russian tea, with delicious, newly-baked white bread; and we felt—as we reclined on the floor among the soft pillows (not knowing then what was in them), sipped hot tea, that had not the usual strong flavour of smoke, and ate white bread, that did not need soaking before we could bite it—that we were indeed in the lap of luxury.   Here the air is not so rarefied and we feel more comfortable.

But we are all suffering from another misery to-day—sunburn—in spite of the amount of face cream and powder we have used. Washing is impossible, and smiling is truly painful. Poor little Sylvia's face is so swollen that her eyes are almost closed, and she looks so comical, but happily it does not seem to worry her much. Both the children are thoroughly happy and contented with their strange life, and are always hungry. There is a little Russian house here for the three Cossacks who look after the Russian Customs. The place is called Karasu; and our march to-day was twenty-five miles—the longest we have done so far; but it was over quite an easy road.

Wednesday, July 8th.—We awoke this morning to find a most glorious summer morning awaiting us, and by seven o'clock we were on our way once more. Our road to-day has been over wonderful meadows, carpeted with flowers. For a long time we marched through an enormously wide valley with a tremendous expanse of grass thick and short, almost like a lawn, that extended on both sides of us for many miles from one mountain range to another. Sometimes a strong odour of onion rose as the horses crushed under their feet the wild onions, sometimes a delightful scent of wild thyme was in the air. The whole scene was so peaceful, and one felt almost as though one was out on a beautiful summer sea. Here and there over this mighty green field were flocks of cattle grazing, looking like tiny black specks compared with the vastness of the plain, and the height of the mountains: a feeling of awe and insignificance comes over one in

the midst of such greatness. Nestling in the shelter
of the little side valleys were the Kirghiz encampments,
in the distance their brown tents looking like a lot of
large fungi, growing on the mountain slopes.

A few years ago these same people were inveterate
highway robbers, making their living out of unfortunate travellers and caravans that passed along this
route. Now they are living peaceful pastoral lives,
and we found them exceedingly hospitable and
courteous. To-day's march has brought us to Akbait, and we have covered about fifteen miles.

Thursday, July 9th.—To-day we have descended
steadily the whole of the march. The road was very
long and it was terribly hot. At one place the ponies
were suddenly attacked by flies, and they suffered a
perfect martyrdom for the rest of the march. And so
did we, for the poor things could do nothing but
jump about with the irritation. One moment my
pony would throw up his head violently to get a fly
off his nose, the next he would dive down to bite one
on his leg, then another would attack his hind leg and
he would try to get at it, and so on, till sometimes
I was afraid he would turn a somersault.

To our surprise and satisfaction, we found in the
tent prepared for us, in addition to the usual Kirghiz
furnishings, a table, stools, and a wooden bed. These
things are not altogether in keeping with a Kirghiz
Ak-oi, but to our depraved European taste, it was
decidedly more comfortable to sit at a table for
dinner, than to crawl about the floor, and sometimes
when reaching for something from the centre of the

table cloth to overbalance into the midst of the dishes and cups with a crash, as we have been doing for the past ten days.

Our camp to-day is at Kara-Ghulak, twenty-two miles from our last.

Friday, July 10th.—We have reached At-Bashi, and have finished our last day on horseback. It has been a hot, tedious march across a great, utterly uninteresting plain. We could see At-Bashi before us the whole time, but seemed to make such slow progress towards it. At last, however, we came to the At-Bashi River, and could see the village distinctly on the other bank, but alas, the flooded river, which looked rather terrifying, rushed along between us and it.

The Russian Aksakal, or headman of the village, and a number of men came across to meet us and help us over, and, after my husband had partaken of the usual cup of Kumiss, offered as a stirrup cup to welcome travellers, we proceeded to cross the river. At first the ford could not be found, and ever so many people went in at different places, but finding that the horses were getting out of their depth, were obliged to come back. At last, after a great deal of shouting and galloping up and down, a ford was decided upon, and we all, about forty of us, plunged in in a body. Nurse and I had a man each side of us holding our arms, and another to lead the pony. My two cavaliers held my arms so tight that once when the three ponies drifted a little apart, I was in danger of being pulled in half. The whole company closed round us in a body to break the force of the water, and with much shouting

for the encouragement of the horses, we at last came
out on the other side a good deal lower down the river
than we had started. The children were wonderfully
calm and brave, and were not frightened by the noise
made by the horses ploughing through the water and
the shouts of the men. But it was a horrid experience,
and I was more than thankful to see everyone come
out safely. Crowds of people were down by the river
to watch us cross, and all the time running through
my mind was Bunyan's wonderful description of
Christian crossing the flood and of the welcome he got
on the other side. The village street was lined with
people, who gazed at us with interest and some
astonishment when they saw the two small children,
and I was just laughing at the excitement we caused,
when Isa, who had Eric with him, called to me :
" Take the Chota Sahib, quick ! I am going to fall."
My husband jumped off his pony and ran to them,
catching Eric just as Isa fell off the other side of the
horse. It gave me a shock, for I began to think what
would have happened if Isa had fainted while we were
in the water. He soon revived in the shade of a tree.
I think he had had a sunstroke, for he had stupidly
ridden all day in the fierce sun with only a thin little
cap on.

The father-in-law of the Aksakal, who had brought
us through the river, had prepared two rooms for us
in his house. He was a Tartar, that is a Russian
Mohammedan from Kazan. The rooms were furnished in European style, and, as we came in from the
heat and glare of the sun, they looked so cool and

homelike, just reminding us of a dear little English cottage.

While we were having tea, a stream of visitors came in to see us, and we held quite an " At Home." Everyone was so friendly and gave us such a hearty welcome, though we were complete strangers. Later on, when the men had finished coming and all was quiet, some of the ladies called on me. The Tartars keep their women very closely shut up and the young and pretty ones are never seen by men outside their own family. While I was entertaining a bevy of really lovely girls, my husband suddenly appeared on the scene : in a moment they had all disappeared like a flock of frightened birds. Our hostess, who is middle-aged, and not at all beautiful, goes about quite freely, and talks to my husband in Russian with perfect self-possession.

Our host and hostess are most kind, and seem as if they cannot do enough for us ; they load the table with good things, and this afternoon the old gentleman entertained us with his gramophone.

The comfort of the pretty rooms, the good beds with sheets and pillow cases, and the nicely cooked food are a real treat after the way we have lived since we left Chini-Bagh.

Our march to-day was twenty miles and a half. The road right from the Turgat Pass is quite good for carts, and here at At-Bashi, it joins the made cart road.

Saturday, July 11th.—After a most blissful night of sleep in comfortable beds, we got up to find a large tarantass, belonging to our host, being prepared for us, and immediately after breakfast we said goodbye to our kind friends and started off at full speed behind three good strong horses. The caravan was left to follow more slowly. We had an exciting drive, doing the thirty miles over a difficult road of hill and dale in four and a half hours. We even crossed a pass, going up and down it on a road not much too wide for the tarantass. At one place we were on a ledge, with a tremendous drop below us. It was not a very comfortable feeling to come down a road of that sort on a loaded vehicle, when the gradient was steep and there was nothing at the edge to save us if the horses had shied or had sent the cart a foot or two towards one side. The last part of the drive was down a deep ravine, and at times the road was so steep that, in spite of having a skid under the wheels, the driver had no control of the horses and was obliged to let them go full speed, regardless of consequences. The horses themselves were marvellously clever, and understood exactly how to manage, and after the first few exciting descents, we gave up worrying ; and in spite of the hairbreath escapes, we could not help but enjoy the drive and the magnificent scenery.

We found a little house prepared for us in Naryn, and a good dinner ready when we arrived in the afternoon. The District Officer called at once to see that we had all we wanted, and altogether the Russians really have been extraordinarily kind and hospitable, and have made all arrangements for our comfort from the moment we entered their territory. Another thirty miles done !

Sunday, July 12th.—To-day we have had a rest from travelling. In the afternoon we had a delightful drive all over Naryn, and were surprised to see how large a place it is. There are a number of good Russian houses, and in the native Bazaar some Russian shops. The inhabitants are a queer mixture of people dressed in the most varied costumes. Russians in smart uniforms walking with fashionably-dressed ladies ; Tartars in long, close-fitting black coats and black fur caps ; natives in their bright-coloured " Chapans " ; and Tunganis and Kirghiz, noticeable by reason of their big fur hats.

We called on a young Russian couple living opposite to us, who have been most kind in supplying us with milk and other necessities. They have a sweet little baby girl of ten months, just like a lovely little doll.

Monday, July 13th.—We went to do some shopping this morning, hoping to find some stores for our onward journey, but were not successful, and to add to our disappointment we discovered that we could only have one tarantass, because the other one kept at this post station was wanted for the mail to Europe. So we must wait patiently till to-morrow.

Tuesday, July 14th.—This morning, at five o'clock, two tarantasses drove up with much noise and clatter to our door, and very soon we had packed ourselves and our belongings into them, and were saying good-bye to Isa, who returns from here to Kashgar. That horrid business is always a wrench for us and for him too, I think. John we are taking on with us to the railway at Aris.

Away we started down the street, making enough noise to wake the whole of Naryn! This sort of driving takes a lot of getting used to, and at first is decidedly nerve-wracking.

On leaving Naryn, we at once plunged into the mountains and drove up hill and down dale, until after three hours of good going, we reached the first station at On Archa, where we stopped to change horses and have some tea. We had one mishap on the road, for just as we were getting near the end of the run, the iron hoop flew off one of the wheels and very shortly after a section of the wheel itself came out. Nurse and Eric, who were in that tarantass, had to come into ours, and the poor old cart just managed to limp very slowly to the post station without the wheel falling to pieces completely.

The second stage was through most wonderful scenery. We drove along an artificial road at the foot of dark pine forests that extended right up the sides of the mountains. The ground was a mass of flowers and purple with wild thyme; and to complete the grandeur of the scene, a mountain torrent rushed and tumbled down over huge boulders just beneath us.

We reached Kara-unkur at two o'clock and decided that we had had enough for the time being of such a novel and exciting mode of travelling. The post station, kept by a *mujik* settler and his family, is simply a log cabin at the foot of the pines, and everything is very primitive and picturesque.

We climbed a high hill in front of the house and found growing amongst the pine trees a marvellous profusion of wild flowers, the colours and quantity of these reminding us of an old English garden. The forget-me-nots were the largest and bluest I have ever seen, and edelweiss was growing a foot high, the blooms of which were very large, and looked as though they were made of pale green velvet. We were coming back laden with flowers when one of the peasant girls belonging to the place came to meet us and begged me to go and see her mother, who had suddenly been taken ill and who they thought was dying. I explained that I was not a doctor, but she implored me to help them. It was rather an awkward position for me, for I could not speak to these people and would have to use our servant John, who spoke Russian, as interpreter, and also I was afraid that if I gave her any medicine and she died afterwards, they would say I had killed her. But I could not be deaf to the appeal, so I went to see her, armed with simple remedies and Elliman's embrocation. The poor woman certainly looked awfully bad, and was in violent pain, and it seemed to me like heart trouble. She was in bed in their little kitchen; the double windows were sealed up; a big fire was burning; something was boiling in a pot; and bread was baking. The heat and atmosphere were stifling; and all the family crowded round the bed, crying and moaning. I insisted on their moving the invalid into another room, where there was some fresh air, and I only allowed the husband to stay in the room. My first remedies gave no relief and several times I thought she was slipping through my hands. Then I started massage with the embrocation, and after a while her colour began to come back and she breathed more freely and finally went to sleep. I left one daughter to watch her mother; and when I went back to the kitchen, there was the rest of the family before the Ikon in the corner, sobbing while they bowed and crossed themselves, and I was so thankful that I had good news for them. How people so utterly ignorant of sick nursing could live in such an isolated place is a mystery to me. One boy of about twelve was sitting with his leg propped up on a chair. I asked what was the matter and was told that some weeks ago he had fallen and broken the limb and they had not had time to take him in to Naryn to get it set.

Wednesday, July 15th.—Our first thought this morning was for my patient, and we were happy to find that she was much better, though still very weak, so we started, after giving the daughter directions about rest and diet.

We began our march by crossing the Dolan Pass. The road was rough and steep, becoming narrower and narrower until we were in a gorge through which a river rushed madly. The pass was crossed without difficulty, for the road was well made and the gradient fairly easy; but the height was sufficient to make us feel symptoms of mountain sickness, and the poor horses puffed and panted painfully. After crossing the pass, the rest of the drive was downhill, and we went at breakneck speed. We are getting quite used to rushing down one hill to get impetus to go up the next, like a switchback railway, and we even enjoy the fun. The *Yamschiks*, as they are called, are very clever, and so far the horses have been good. The children are enjoying it all immensely, and when we stop at a post station to change horses, are like little wild animals let out of a cage.

We have only managed to do two stages again to-day, as we could not get horses to take us on, and had perforce to put up at Kumbelata, where we found the people most surly and disobliging. We have just had a grand tussle with them over a tough old hen, for which they wanted to charge double the regulation price, which should be about tenpence.

Thursday, July 16th.—We tried to make a very early start this morning and were on the road by six o'clock. But alas ! we had only gone about half an hour, when the wheel of one of the carts broke down, and we had to sit and wait while one of the drivers unharnessed a horse and galloped back for another wheel, and so lost a precious hour. We reached Kutemaldi, on the Issykul Lake, after stopping at the intermediate station, at two p.m., just as a thunderstorm came on. So far we have not had a drop of rain during our marches all the way from Kashgar, and the temperature is simply perfect ; cool at night, and comfortably warm during the day. This morning we even had frost.

Kutemaldi is a tiny village, consisting of a few houses and a telegraph office ; and it is the junction of the Naryn and Vyernyi roads. Strange that even the telegraph poles after our absence from civilization of nearly five years looked homelike !

We found empty rooms in the post station and took possession of them, but just as we were preparing to go to bed, a Russian officer with his wife and two children and nursemaid arrived, and almost at the same time two Poles. We wondered how we were to pass the night with such a crowd in two rooms, and were greatly relieved when the Poles got horses and went on, and the Russian family found other quarters, and left us in peace.

To-morrow morning we shall have a race to see which of us can be ready soonest, so as to be the first to procure the horses at the next small station.

Tuesday, July 17*th.*—This morning we got up in a great hurry, rushed through our breakfast and packing, seeing all the time our opponents, who were in a house immediately opposite, doing the same. Unfortunately we had most to do, and just as we were ready to start, they drove past us, smiling triumphantly. Our drivers thoroughly entered into the competition, for the party who got to the next station first would have the first chance of fresh horses to go on with. What a race we did have, flying up and down the hills after them. Once we actually caught them up on a very steep hill, but we could not pass, as the road was too narrow. When they got to the top, away they flew down again and our carts being heavier could never manage to get ahead. Even the horses seemed to understand the fun and went like the wind. But it was all to no purpose, for when we reached the station we found that there were no horses for anybody there, and at midday there would be only three ready, which the Russians might just as well have, for they were no use to us when we wanted nine. So we made friends with our adversaries and spent a very pleasant time together till they started off again. At about four o'clock we got our horses and drove on through the Burman defile, an exceedingly wild gorge with the River Chu, which at this time is in full flood, rushing madly through it.

Saturday, July 18th.—To-day's stages have been long and tiring, over rough and stony roads. We have left the mountains with the cool air and are now on what is known as the *steppes*. It had been very hot and dusty, and it was such a relief to get into the shady roads of Tokmak.

Tokmak is more like a large native bazaar than a Russian town.

Sunday, July 19th.—To-day we have managed to do three stages for the first time, fifty-five miles altogether. We reached Pishpek, a large Russian town, early in the afternoon, and after a little rest and stroll through the streets, started off again and drove one more stage before bedtime, putting up for the night in a tiny village called Sukalak. To-day's journey across the *steppes* has been full of interest; for the whole way we have been driving through tiny villages of Russian settlers, who seem to have taken possession of the land that used to belong to the Kirghiz. The latter have been driven out and evidently from what we have heard bitterly resent it. These villages are

very pretty, with their shady lanes and thatched
cottages. Huge haystacks are everywhere, and
splendid cattle. The fields are under cultivation, and
harvesting machines are at work. Evidently many of
the families had only just arrived ; for they were living
in booths made of branches of trees in the most
primitive fashion, while the houses were being built.
Jolly-looking women and girls in print frocks, with
bright handkerchiefs over their heads, were doing the
building while the men were working in the fields.

Monday, July 20th.—Our march to-day has been
exceedingly disagreeable on account of the awful dust.
At times we could see nothing around us, even the
horses were obliterated by the clouds that completely
enveloped us. We had intended doing three stages ;
but when we reached the second station, it was already
getting late and we had had no dinner. So we put up
for the night at Kara-Balti, a pretty enough village,
but swarming with flies.

Tuesday, July 21st. The dust again to-day has been
suffocating and all our belongings are getting ruined.
I opened one of the boxes and found that the dust
had penetrated quite halfway down. What will be
the condition of our things when we reach home ?

The food question is a most difficult one ; and if
we had not brought a good supply of stores, and John
to cook for us, I do not know what we should have
done. All the post stations are supposed to have meat
for travellers, but there is seldom any to be found
when it is wanted ; and the eggs, when we manage
to procure any, are far from fresh. We can always get

plenty of bread, but the Russians like their bread quite sour, and it does not agree with the children, or in fact with any of us.

Wednesday, July 22nd.—This morning we tried to make a very early start and rose at daybreak, hoping to be able to rest during the great heat of the day. Just as we were ready to go, a tarantass containing a lady and gentleman and a little girl drove up. They wanted horses, but we had taken all, so the lady came and begged us to let them have one span, because she was in a great hurry to get to St. Petersburg to her mother who, as she said, was ill. Reluctantly we had to refuse, for we were all ready to start, and we too were anxious to get on for the sake of the children. At the next station they caught us up while we were having a meal ; but again we started off and left them waiting for horses.

In the evening, as we were sitting down to supper, who should appear but the same party. We did not intend going on, so they got their horses at once, meaning to travel all night. The Russians seem to be able to sleep while they are being rattled along the road. I found that the lady spoke French, and while they were waiting for the horses to be changed, I had a talk with her. She told me she was a widow and that her husband had been killed in a bomb outrage in Russia ; but it was strange that she never mentioned a word about her mother being ill, and simply said she was taking her little girl to school in St. Petersburg. So my conscience feels clearer now, for I believe the other story was made up on the spur of the moment—

all day I have been feeling rather mean about not letting her have the horses.

The last stage to-day was simply a chapter of accidents. We had three rather wild horses in our tarantass, which, soon after starting, bolted. Away we flew down the road at an awful pace, the driver pulling with all his might at the reins, but with no effect whatever, until he drove us up a steep bank at the side of the road, and so brought the animals to a standstill. After that we had to go very slowly and carefully so as not to excite them; but we were only about half a mile from the post station when they took fright at some carts we were passing, and bolted again. Just at that moment we were caught in a sudden whirl-wind and could see nothing around us for dust, and that scared the poor beasts still more. This time we were saved by one of the wheels flying off, and we were tipped on to one side. The axle dragging on the road acted as a brake, and the horses stopped. The driver stuck the wheel on with a rusty nail, and we finished the journey at a walking pace, feeling thoroughly tired and shaken.

Thursday, July 23rd.—We have beaten the record to-day and have done four stages, reaching Aulie-ata at about four o'clock this afternoon. Poor little Eric has been so ill all day with fever; but the travelling has not seemed to worry him much, for he has slept the most of the time in spite of the jolting. Our road has been across the grassy *steppes* and the dust was not so bad. Aulie-ata is a large town, more native than Russian.

We started our adventures this morning by losing a wheel again, which was not to be wondered at, seeing that the driver only put it on with a rusty nail yesterday and never thought of mending it properly before starting this morning; but one gets used to such trifles as shedding wheels on a journey of this sort. We had heard so much of the terrific heat we should have here, but have been pleasantly surprised, for it has not been at all unbearable.

Friday, July 24th.—To our great relief, Eric got up much better this morning, so I hope it was only a passing feverish attack. As usual at the large post stations, they were very slow in getting our horses harnessed, and it was eight before we started. The day was beautifully clear and the snow mountains showing through the trees made a pretty picture in the morning light. For some distance we drove through enormous hay fields, where the peasants were hard at work tossing and stacking the hay. It was a merry scene, and quite homelike. We were all so tired and hungry after doing our three stages that, although we heard that we might have difficulty in getting horses in the morning, we felt we must risk a delay to get a good rest. This place is called Kulbastai.

Saturday, July 25th.—Another day of jolting and dust. We shall be thankful when this part of the journey is over, for we are all heartily sick of this mode of life. This post station goes by the name of Kornilovski.

Sunday, July 26th.—To-day's march has been done with the greatest difficulty, for the children have both been very unwell and can take no food whatever.

They have not seemed themselves for some days and to-day they have been downright ill. To make matters worse, I suddenly had an attack of fever come on, which decided us to stop at the end of our second stage at Beli-Voda. Eric and I had to go to bed, or rather to lie down on hard wooden sofas, and it was pitiable to see poor little Sylvia. She was so ill and miserable and yet wanted to run about the whole time, and seemed as though she could not rest. There was little peace for anyone, for we could only have the tiny inner room that was reserved for ladies, to ourselves. The whole afternoon travellers were arriving and having tea in the next room, talking and laughing and making a distracting noise. Happily we had the place to ourselves for the night.

I am much better this evening, but the children seem to be getting steadily worse and we are becoming anxious about them.

We had one exciting experience to-day that came near to being a tragedy. Coming down a steep hill, the driver lost control of the horses in the luggage cart—it was much too heavily loaded and they simply could not hold it back. They dashed down the hill at an alarming speed, and only just missed smashing into the tarantass Eric and Nurse were in by a hair's breadth. At the bottom of the hill was a narrow bridge, but just before they reached it three wheels flew off and the horses were brought to a standstill and no further damage was done. But these things upset one when one is not feeling over fit.

Monday, July 27th.—The little ones were so ill all

night that we got up at daybreak and hastened into Chimkent, where we heard there was a doctor. We drove straight to his house and fortunately found him in. He says we must stay a few days here till they are better and has found us rooms in a sort of inn quite near his house, and next door to a chemist's shop. It is delightfully cool and restful here, after the hot dusty roads, and a few days' rest will, I hope, set us all up. The first thing we did was to give the children a warm bath, put them into clean clothes and get them to bed. They looked so utterly dirty and wretched when we arrived that I felt I must cry; and they were asleep as soon as they got between clean sheets and slept the whole day through,—a sleep of exhaustion. Both of them have lost weight in the last few days.

July 28th to August 23rd.—Our two or three days here have lengthened out into nearly a month, and a time of awful anxiety it has been. The children, instead of recovering in a few days, developed dysentery, and to add to our troubles Nurse took it too. For three weeks it was a fight for Eric's life and several times we thought we would lose him. Sylvia, though bad enough, was not as desperately ill as Eric; and Nurse had a comparatively light attack. My husband and I did all the nursing and during that time we neither of us had a single night's rest, just snatching a few minutes' sleep at odd times. The Russian doctor was extraordinarily kind, often coming in three or four times a day, and doing his utmost to procure anything we wanted for our comfort. There were others too who, simply hearing that we were strangers and in trouble, were most helpful in sending us goat's milk, cake, fruit, and delicacies. It is when one is in such straits as we were that one discovers how many kind people there are in the world. But I never imagined that anyone could receive so much sympathy and practical help from perfect strangers as we did during all that anxious month.

Still it was all very difficult, for we had only two small rooms, with no space in them for beds for my husband and myself, and our choice of sleeping place was limited to an uncomfortable sofa and the floor. Our landlady was the only person who would have us, because of the fear of infection. But to nurse such serious illness under these conditions has not been an easy job.

Chimkent is a delightful little place to stay in. The town is divided into two parts, the Russian and native. There are about half a dozen Russian shops, a military hospital, barracks, and a church ; while the native bazaar is quite large. Also there are numerous spirit shops frequented by both Russians and natives. The surrounding country is beautiful. Just on the outskirts of the town are some picturesque little bits of wooded scenery, while beyond lie the vast *steppes* of Russia,—great stretches of grassy plain, where even on the hottest day one can find a fresh breeze blowing. It is much cooler here than in Kashgar at this time of the year, and we are very fortunate to have been delayed in a place with a good climate.

The little ones have so far recovered for us to try to continue our journey to-morrow to the railway at

Aris. They are awfully weak still and are just shadows of their former selves. Poor little Eric cannot even stand by himself, but it is best to try and get home as quickly as possible.

August 23rd.—This morning, at the early hour of 2.30, we got up so as to be off at dawn, in the hope of reaching our halfway halt, while it was yet cool. We packed the carts by starlight, and as day broke we drove out of the inn gates and down the avenue which constituted the main road, thus taking farewell of Chimkent while it was still sleeping. Our landlord drove my husband, Sylvia and me in a huge travelling tarantass of his own, while his servant was in charge of a smaller one, in which were Nurse, Eric, and our landlady, who had come with us for a little holiday, with John on the box alongside the driver. We did the first stage at a very good pace and stayed through the heat of the day in a little village at the house of a *mujik* family. They were evidently very poor, hard-working people, and everything in the house was of the simplest, though delightfully clean. But what struck us most forcibly were the beautiful and costly Ikons, or holy pictures, put up in a corner of each room. The Russians are, I think, in their hearts a deeply religious people and will stint themselves to pay for an expensive Ikon, before which they go to pray for help in every difficulty or trouble in their daily life.

At half-past four we started again, having about twenty miles still to go. We wanted to be off sooner, in case any delay should occur on the road, but our landlord would not get ready, and kept saying that there was plenty of time. About half an hour after we started some part of the harness broke, and we had to wait a good while for that to be mended. Then the road became bad, and compelled us to slacken speed, till at last the darkness was on us, and we were still out on the *steppes*. To make matters worse, the ground began to be full of ruts, which, after we had nearly turned over in one of them, made our driver so nervous that he insisted on walking ahead while his servant drove our cart, and John took charge of the other one behind. He struck matches now and again to see the road, but these were soon exhausted. It was a horrible experience,—there out in the pitch darkness with no lantern, afraid to go on for fear of driving into some big hole. And to add to our anxiety, Eric was running a high temperature again. At one place we were obliged to get out while they drove down a steep incline and up on the other side. It was a risk to take Eric out of the cart where we had been keeping him very warm, into the cool wind. But that seemed better than the probability of being smashed up in the darkness. That last twenty miles took us not less than six hours to do, and we reached Aris at ten-thirty, to find Mons. and Mme. Minkeldi, with whom we were to stay, already in bed, and the house shut up. But they were very kind in getting beds ready for us and doing everything possible to make us comfortable. It was midnight before we got to rest, all utterly worn out.

We have travelled nearly eight hundred miles by road from Kashgar.

August 24th.—Poor little Eric has had a day of suffering. The fever is running very high and some of the old symptoms have come back. Our host and hostess are just kindness itself, and it is such a pleasure to be in a civilized household once again. They have three jolly little children, but they must be kept away from ours for fear of infection. In a country like this, one must take every precuation against dysentery.

It seems strange to find such a beautiful European house, furnished and decorated with refined artistic taste. The garden is lovely with flowers, great masses of bamboos, palms, and all sorts of uncommon trees. In the centre, a fountain is playing, and sprays are kept going for watering purposes. We were very surprised to learn that there is no natural water and very little rain, and the whole garden is kept alive with water that has been brought from a great distance by train and pumped up into a huge elevated tank erected beside the railway line. Mons. Minkeldi is Chief Engineer and Controller of this section of the Tashkent-Moscow Railway.

Aris itself is a very small place, consisting of a handful of houses for the railway people, a little native bazaar, and the Station—all beyond is desert. This afternoon Nurse and I took Sylvia on to the Station to see the train to Moscow go through. We nearly wept with delight and excitement at seeing a train again after all these years. Sylvia, though, was rather scared at such a monster.

August 25th.—Eric's temperature is normal to-day, and he is much brighter, so we have decided, in spite of Mme. Minkeldi's pressing invitation to stay longer, to leave by this afternoon's train.

September 7th.—At last our long journey is over, and we are at home. It is more than three months since we left Kashgar, and in that time we have had many strange experiences. The children steadily improved and grew stronger after leaving Aris, though even now they show the effects of their illness.

We came on quickly through Samara to Moscow, where we rested one day. Then viâ Warsaw to Berlin, where we passed four most delightful days with our old Kashgar friend, Dr. A. von Le Coq, and his wife and family. And lastly, from Berlin to London viâ Calais and Dover. It was a beautiful calm afternoon when we left Calais, with our eyes fixed on the faint coast line before us, ever growing more clear and distinct, till at last Dover Castle rose majestically above the white cliffs and green slopes. Only those who, like us, have been exiled from the home-land for many years, can enter into our feelings of joy and thankfulness that the end of a long journey was at last within reach.

CHAPTER XII

THE CHINESE REVOLUTION

In the Spring of 1912, disconcerting talk and rumours of revolution began floating about. News came of Chinese Ambans being assassinated in cities away across the Province towards Inner China. The trouble flared up first in one place and then in another; but always coming nearer to Kashgar, until the Kashgar officials began to get nervous; and at last hid themselves in their Yamêns and even in their cellars. On Sunday, May 5th, my husband went to see Yu-en Tao-tai, who had been in hiding, and practically a prisoner in his Yamên for weeks. He knew perfectly well that he would be the first to suffer if the flame broke out in Kashgar.

My husband was surprised to find him much happier, going freely about his Yamên; and the Tao-tai told him that he and other Ambans had given large amounts of money to the revolutionary party, and they hoped that things were settled. My husband's private opinion was that it was just the beginning of a long course of blackmail.

The Tao-tai showed him a jade bangle he was wearing, saying: " You see this beautiful of piece of jade— it is perfect, without a flaw or crack in it. So long as it remains as it is now, my life is safe while I wear it."

My husband came home and was telling me all this, while we were having tea in the garden ; and just as he was speaking, someone came running with the news that the storm had broken in Ak-su, the next big city to the north-east of Kashgar, and that all the Ambans were murdered. We knew then that it would soon reach us and wondered about the poor old Tao-tai's jade bangle.

Two days later on Tuesday morning, May 7th, we were wakened at four a.m. by our servant, who said that a Cossack had come to say that Mons. Sokoff, the Russian Consul, was on his way to us. We guessed the reason of his early visit at once ; in fact before going to bed the servant, whose duty it was to keep guard by the strong room in the office, had come to my husband to ask if he might have someone else with him and also whether they could not have revolvers, because of the excitement and talk there was in the city : they were thoroughly nervous.

My husband jumped up at once, dressed himself and tried to stuff his revolver in his pocket without my seeing it. He told me to dress myself and the children and rouse the household. My brother-in-law, Donald, was staying with us, also Mr. Hunter, of the China Inland Mission.

In a few minutes Mons. Sokoff and some of the Russian officers arrived with the news that a fight was going on in the city at the moment, and that all the gates were closed and no one knew exactly what was happening.

It is very strange what silly ideas one has at really

critical moments. My one thought was that the children and I must be in clean clothes if we were to be murdered, and to the surprise of the Russians, we all appeared at 4.30 a.m. as though we were going to a garden party, in spotless white !

We heard a few shots fired, but otherwise everything was deadly quiet, and it seemed impossible that on that peaceful summer morning anything horrible could be happening.

At last, just as we were sitting down to breakfast, a man who was a representative of the revolutionaries appeared on the city wall waving a red card, which he threw down to one of our servants, who ran out to him, with the message that several of the Ambans were killed, among them the poor old Tao-tai (in spite of the jade bangle), his wife and the Hsien-Kuan. He said we were not to be alarmed, as we Europeans would be safe, but all the same we had better stay at home for a few days as the people were excited and out of hand. It was simply an affair between the Chinese themselves.

So we put up all the British flags we could find and had five flying round the compound ; then my husband gave orders to the British subjects to do the same on their houses. As they had none ready, they set-to with feverish haste to manufacture Union Jacks, and some very queer specimens they turned out.

Mr. Hunter was dressed as a Chinaman, with his own hair in a pigtail, and my husband insisted on his cutting off that appendage and dressing as a European. Otherwise he might be mistaken for a Chinaman and get murdered. He was a big, tall man and none of my husband's things would fit him, so we sent to Mr. Högberg for a suit of his clothes and a hat, as they were of the same build; and we turned Mr. Hunter into what he really was—a splendid Scotchman.

About midday one of the city gates was opened, and a number of Chinese refugee officials got out and came to us, hidden in carts driven by natives who had befriended them. We took them in, giving them some rooms in the garden, putting up tents when the rooms were full, till we had as many as we had accommodation for. They were all in a state of terror, for the roads were infested with the revolutionaries, who were going about flourishing horrible three-edged swords, on which were gruesomely suggestive stains.

The widow and little son of the murdered Hsien-Kuan were among the first to be brought to us. She, poor thing, was in a pitiable plight, for she had seen her husband literally hacked to death, and when they took the boy to kill him, she threw herself on his assailants, imploring them to spare him, and they, having bigger game to pursue, let him go. She kept wailing: "I saw it all, and the picture will always be before me." One poor woman had a baby only a few days old, and the shock upset her so badly that she could not feed it. I gave her bottles and food (for our own youngest boy was not a year old) and while she remained with us, very ill most of the time, the baby throve. Several officials on whose heads there were big prices, came and lived in tents in the garden for many weeks.

Five days after all this happened, late at night two of the Swedish missionaries came to us with a very miserable-looking man dressed like a native and being carried by their servant on his back. When they got him safely into our house, my husband discovered that he was an official who had been missing since that fateful Tuesday morning. He was a man who had oppressed the people when he was in power and the mob was mad to have him and declared that no amount of money would save his life. The poor thing was half demented, for he had been hidden by a kindly native baker in his mud oven for five days, with only a bit of bread now and again to eat, that the baker had managed to smuggle in to him. It would have been impossible for us to protect a man with his record for we had no guard whatever. The only place where he might be safe was at the Russian Consulate, where they had about sixty Cossacks.

So, after giving him some food, my husband and his brother smuggled him across the fields and got him safely into the hands of the Russians. He was locked up in a room at once, and was never seen until some weeks later he emerged disguised as a Cossack and was sent to Russia with two real Cossacks carrying the mail, and from there he got home to China.

When the mob could not find him on the day of the murders, they took his little boy to kill him instead. Some brute brought his sword down on the child's head, making a fearful gash. The mother fought like a mad thing for her child and rescued him, fleeing with him to some kindly natives, who hid them under a lot

of fodder on the house top, and thus the poor things
stayed for days in the summer heat. Nothing was
done for the child's wound, and it festered and was
attacked by flies till it was a moving mass of maggots.

The Swedish nurses hearing from some patient about
this poor Chinese woman and child, bravely went into
the city and searched till they found them, and got
them smuggled out to their hospital, where, after long
patient treatment, the child recovered and the wound
completely healed up. Then with a number of other
Chinese women and children, they were sent back to
China. The woman had no idea what had become of
her husband, and thought he was killed. Imagine
what was the joy of husband and wife when they met
many months after in their old home in Hunan all
safe and well. But there were not many stories that
had such a happy ending as this one.

The day after the revolution broke out in the Old
City, Yang-Ta-jen, the Hsie-tai, was at our house,
discussing the state of affairs with my husband. He
was one of the very few Ambans left alive. Suddenly
a man came rushing in with the news that the Chinese
City was in an uproar, and the Ambans there were
being assassinated. The Hsie-tai rushed out, jumped
on his horse, and galloped off to the New City, with
a few men. When he reached the gate, he found an
excited mob with a Chinaman in their midst whom they
were going to kill. The Hsie-tai asked what the man
had done. " He has cut off his pigtail," was the reply.
The Hsie-tai pulled off his own cap, saying : " See, I
have cut off mine, you must kill me first, then you can

kill him." They so admired his pluck that they kow-towed, saying that they could not lay hands on a brave man. "Then let that poor wretch go too," he said, and they did. He found that they had already murdered some of the Ambans, though the Ti-tai was still alive in hiding in his Yamên.

That same afternoon a telegram was sent from the New City, saying that the mob had got quite out of hand, and was marching to the Old City to loot and burn, and that they would not respect the Europeans.

So we knew that we had to prepare for the worst. The British subjects were told to bring their valuables and stow them away in the room that could be best defended, and where we were all to go to, if necessary. My husband and his brother even arranged between them how we women and children were to be dis-patched if the mob was too strong for us, though this I did not know till long afterwards. Rolls of bandages were prepared, and I packed up the children's clothes and the baby's food into bags in case we found it necessary to run and hide in a place we had already decided upon.

Our servants armed themselves with any kind of weapon they could find,—knives, sticks, old swords, etc.,—and even our governess, Miss Cresswell, took the big carving knife and steel to bed with her. After-wards we heard that one of the Swedish nurses had armed herself with a big syringe full of acid that would blind a crowd of people for days if she sprayed them with it. Quite a good weapon for protection ! Having made all preparations possible, we lay down fully

dressed, while Donald and Mr. Hunter took it in turns
to do sentry duty round the house and garden.

There was no chance of sleep, but it was something
to be able to lie down after the day we had been
through. All was strangely quiet, and we were getting
drowsy, when at midnight three cannons boomed out,
making the house vibrate. Up we jumped, and everyone came running, thinking that the attack had begun.
We waited and waited, and nothing more happened
till at last the cocks began to crow, the birds twittered,
and then the old sun shone once more. The relief of
hearing natural sounds after a night of such nervous
strain is past description. Afterwards we learnt
that the mob had started out from the New City,
but for some unknown reason turned back. The
only explanation I can give is in Tennyson's words :
" More things are wrought by prayer than this world
dreams of." And this was not the only case in which
we had the same experience. Several times outrages
were planned to take place in the night, and failed.
The cannons that had disturbed us were salutes being
fired by the Tao-tai's murderers when his body was put
into the coffin with due ceremony. The men who had
murdered his old wife were very much blamed by the
rest of the party for touching a woman, but they said
that in the dim light of the dawn they had mistaken
her for her husband.

About a week after all this took place in Kashgar, the
revolutionary movement had spread to Yangi-Hissar,
two days' journey towards Yarkand. Plans were
made to assassinate the Amban there on a certain day,

and he was living in terror. On this very day an exceptionally severe dust storm, or *buran* came on. It passed over Kashgar, leaving us in darkness, and was seen to be approaching Yangi-Hissar across the desert. The pillar of dust looked so unusual that the people got nervous; and when pitch darkness came over the city, blacker than they had ever known it before with a buran; and a wind so violent that no one could stand against it; they decided that the gods were displeased about the proposed murder and postponed it. Before their courage had returned, orders from the revolutionary government in Kashgar came, forbidding any more assassinations, and so the man's life was saved, and no more blood was shed.

Right from the first, my husband and Donald rode through the city unattended, to show the Chinese that we believed their word when they said we should be safe. Nothing impresses the Chinese so much as to show that one has no fear. They were not at all hostile, so Donald asked me to let Eric, who was about nine then, ride with him one day, and Eric of course was delighted at the prospect of going through the City. I, it must be confessed, was not so pleased, but I thought if it would help to improve the feeling of confidence, he must go. When they got in amongst the soldiers, Donald was rather alarmed, for they crowded round Eric, stopping his pony. But it was only their pleasure at seeing the child, for they greeted him in a friendly way, bringing him sweets and cakes, the real Chinese love of children coming out in these very men who had been doing such brutal deeds. After that, they took their ride regularly right through the camp of soldiers, and were never molested.

Our two elder children, who were old enough to know something of what was going on, though they did not know the full seriousness of the time we were passing through, did not worry much. They had such perfect confidence in their father's power to put everything right. Miss Cresswell, too, was always calm and resourceful. What unnerved me most was to see the little ones peacefully asleep, when my tiresome imagination would run on what might happen before morning.

This state of affairs went on for two months. The country was ruled by a pork butcher and a barber, and the few Ambans that were left were completely in their hands. The Consuls refused to recognize them, though they were very anxious to make friends with my husband and Mons. Sokoff.

So we went on, with our refugees still with us. Their assailants would come right up to our gate after them but dare not go under the British Flag, though they knew perfectly well that we had no one armed to resist them. Our splendid Union Jacks flew round us for six months or more and we loved them for all they stood for.

After the most critical time had passed, the Ti-tai from the New City screwed up courage to drive over to see us. He was escorted by a crowd of soldiers of the new régime. I went in to see him, as I knew his wife and also we wanted to show special friendliness towards him. He asked me if I had not been very much upset and nervous during the revolution. "No," I said, "why should I be when you Chinese had promised that we should be safe?" He seemed rather pleased. "Besides," said my husband, "though you could so easily have killed us all, you would have had the British Government to reckon with afterwards, which would not have been so simple for you." Turning to the soldiers who were crowding in at the door, he said: "There, do you hear that? Don't you ever forget that the British Government will make you responsible for the lives of these people." They all nodded solemnly at each other. It was so childish altogether; and they looked so solemn and yet so comical that we could hardly keep a serious expression.

After about two months a Russian regiment arrived to police the country.

We still had some excitements when through misunderstandings and excess of military zeal on the part of the Russians, they and the Chinese came near to serious fighting. Of course, we personally, felt much safer after the Russian troops came, and their presence had the effect of keeping the country quiet. But I fancy the military people thought that they had been brought there under false pretences, and that a life of peace and monotony was not at all to their taste. The day the troops arrived the Russian Consul arranged a grand reception for them in a garden some miles from Kashgar on the edge of the oasis to which all we Europeans were invited.

After the time of strain we had been through it may be imagined what a thrill it gave us to see a cavalry regiment, led by the band, marching towards us across the desert.

The officers were dismounting, and introductions were being made, when to everyone's surprise up drove the Ti-tai and several of the new revolutionary officials, who greeted the Russians with the utmost friendliness.

As a matter of fact, my husband had advised the Ti-tai that, as it was unwise for him to oppose the arrival of the Russians, the next best thing was to treat them as honoured guests.

The Colonel in command turned to my husband and said : " But what is the meaning of this ? We understood that we should have to fight our way into Kashgar, and instead we are received like old friends ! "

The greater part of the regiment camped in the country a few miles out of Kashgar, while the remainder augmented the Consulate guard.

But the valiant fighting men soon found life very dull and monotonous, and small fights began to take place between drunken Cossacks and Chinese soldiers. Then, one night just as we were preparing to retire, a messenger came running from the Russian Consul with the startling news that the City gate was going to be blown open, and we must be prepared for some excitement and probably heavy fighting. This is what had caused the Russians to decide on such drastic measures !—Earlier in the evening, before the City gate was shut at sunset, a party of Cossacks was wandering about the bazaars on horseback. It happened to be the special day in the year when the Chinese were wont to burn paper money before certain

shrines for the benefit of those who had departed
this life. The Cossacks, interested in the ceremony,
got off their horses, and left them standing untethered,
while they stood near to watch. They noticed that
the fire made by the burning paper was rather
dangerously near a Russian house, and remonstrated
with the Chinese, who told them to mind their own
business. This started a heated argument, which
made the Cossacks forget about their horses. Suddenly
there came a sharp peal of thunder that startled the
animals, and away they bolted through the narrow
streets, out of the gate, and straight home to their
stables at the Consulate. It was just the hour of
sunset, when the City closed its doors, and the great
iron gate was shut behind them, imprisoning the
Cossacks for the night.

When the riderless horses arrived home, someone
ran to the Consul with the news. He wrung his hands
and exclaimed " Oh, my poor Cossacks, they have
been trapped in the City, and will be massacred ! We
must rescue them."

The troops were at once sent for from camp, and
they came galloping in, full of importance, for at last
they were to have a fight and thus justify their
existence. At about midnight they blew a great hole
round the lock of the gate, and it was opened.

All evening a violent thunderstorm had been raging,
and the rain was coming down in torrents, but un-
daunted, the troops galloped into the city to find not
a soul about. It was like a city of the dead, for everyone was in bed, or under shelter from the storm, and

the Cossacks who had made all the trouble were
spending a gay night in a teashop, with no idea of the
excitement they were causing, and were not found till
next morning.

But some demonstration had to be made, so the
Colonel posted a number of men in the chief market
square, sent some up to the roof of the mosque,
thereby offending the Mullahs, and others patrolled
the streets, and hunted for the lost Cossacks. And so
they passed the night in the drenching rain.

The Chinese officials who were safe away from the
storm in their well built *yamêns* knew nothing of
these happenings till next morning, when to their
surprise and indignation, they found their City gate
blown open, and the place occupied by Russian
soldiers.

The Ti-tai came at once to see my husband. " What
is the meaning of all this," he asked indignantly. " It
looks very much like a declaration of war, and I have
given orders for our guns to be run up on the city
wall and trained on to the Russian Consulate."

My husband always advised the Chinese to give no
provocation whatever to the Russians, or they would
just play into their hands, so he told the Ti-tai that
the best thing he could do was to countermand that
order, and to treat the incident as a mistake on the
part of the Russians, which it very evidently was.

The matter ended, by the Russians mending the
gate !

The Chinese at last decided to transfer some of the
revolutionary soldiers to Urumtchi, the capital of the

New Dominion, and it was arranged that they were to march out of the city late one night in the Autumn of 1912, by the north gate, and along the Maralbashi road. This had been freely talked about all day in the bazaars; so it was hardly possible that the Russians had not heard of it.

After dinner that evening, my husband and his brother were walking along the road past the Russian Consulate, and were surprised to see the whole regiment of Cossacks mounted and ready to march. My husband strolled up to the Consul, who was talking to the Colonel, and remarked on the smartness of the men, and asked casually what they were doing marching out so late in the evening. The Consul replied that they were going out to have some manœuvres on the Maralbashi road, as they had not had enough exercise lately.

The Maralbashi road was the very one that the Chinese troops were to take, and what was more likely than that the two regiments, meeting in the dark, should come to fighting?

My husband came home and sent a servant off at once with a message to the Chinese that he was surprised that they should send out their troops at night, without officially notifying the foreign Consuls. The Russian Cossacks were out on the Maralbashi road having manœuvres, and there might very easily be an accident in the dark!

Very shortly a Chinese servant arrived with the Ti-tai's red card, and the message that the plans had been changed, and that now it was decided to march

the Chinese troops out at 8 o'clock next morning
by the East gate ! The man then went on and gave
the same message to the Russian Consul.

Next morning the Cossacks came home in not the
best of spirits, having sat waiting all night for the
Chinese soldiers. Thus a collision was avoided.

It transpired afterwards that the revolution which
had spread over the whole of China had been engi-
neered by an enormous Secret Society that had
extensive ramifications in all the provinces.

People of every rank and class belonged to it, from
the highest to the lowest, and the Hsie-tai of Kashgar
was strongly suspected of being a member, and for
that reason he survived when his fellow Ambans were
murdered, and played a great role when the country
was in the hands of the revolutionaries. The great aim
and object of the Secret Society seemed to be to wrench
the government with its money-making possibilities
out of the hands that held it, and to hold it themselves.
Gradually things quieted down. The old régime got
the upper hand once more. The pork butcher, and
the barber were beheaded, and their followers became
good citizens. But many of the Chinese officials
who survived had had to pay very dearly for their
lives, with the money they had extorted from the
people.

The revolutionaries studiously avoided interfering
with foreigners, and hardly any British or Russian
subjects suffered loss through them. The object my
husband had in view was to prevent any collision
between them and the Russian troops, and thanks to

the influence which the late Sir George Buchanan, then our Ambassador at St. Petersburg, was able to exert on the Russian Foreign Office, the troops were withdrawn after an occupation of Kashgar, which had lasted the best part of two years.

CHAPTER XIII

CHANGES IN KASHGAR

WITH the passing of the years, life in Kashgar had changed in many ways and, during the last period of five years that I spent there, conditions were very different from what they were when I first went out.

Our youngest boy, Robin, was born in 1911, so now we had three children, with a governess, Miss Annie Cresswell, in charge of the education of the two eldest.

In 1913, the new British Consulate-General, designed by our old friend, Mr. Högberg, and built by an army of native workmen, was finished. The work had been in preparation for some years, for everything had to be done from the very beginning. The trees, selected while they were still growing in different parts of the country, were felled, skinned, and allowed to season in the sun of several summers ; bricks were made, and dried in the sun or baked in kilns, and fittings collected gradually from Europe.

The first buildings to be put up were a row of three small houses intended for the Munshis, and the Hospital Assistant. Into these we moved, while our home and the office buildings were being demolished and rebuilt on almost the same spot as the old house had been ;

though not quite so perilously near the edge of the cliff. The cliff itself was built up and strengthened with a good brick wall.

The Consulate was a fine building, still of the bungalow type, with the exception of the towers, which overlooked the garden and in which there were two upstair rooms and a loggia commanding a splendid view over the whole country. The roof was flat and a veritable sun trap, greatly appreciated in winter, when we could mostly get a glorious panorama of the magnificent Pamir Mountains from it.

Inside, the large reception rooms opened out of a central hall and could be shut off from our private part of the house. That would not appeal much to people at home, but in Kashgar, when my husband was entertaining Chinese visitors with their swarms of curious followers, it was a very great convenience.

The whole house was centrally heated by hot air circulating in all the rooms from a furnace in a hot air chamber running under the house, and in winter it proved beautifully warm and comfortable.

Paper-hanging was rather a difficulty, for the native workman could not manage it at all ; but it was solved by the whole Swedish colony coming to our assistance, and about a dozen of us of both sexes set to and papered nine rooms in three days ; which was not such bad going, I think, for amateurs.

I had a big airy kitchen, with a good kitchener made of brick and iron, also designed by Mr. Högberg, dairy, store rooms, and laundry. All so different from my first little dark hole of a kitchen, in which the oven was a round iron box placed on glowing charcoal, with some bits of charcoal on the lid. But all the same I must give that box the credit of baking cakes, and even bread wonderfully well, though the cook was often nearly asphyxiated by the fumes of the charcoal.

Office buildings worthy of a Consulate, comprised several offices ; a large court room, in which hung a good picture of our King ; and in the centre—with the rooms built round it to protect it from thieves getting in from outside—was the strong room.

Over the main gateway stood a splendid Coat of Arms sent out to us by the British Foreign Office, and of which we were immensely proud. The whole property, enclosed by a high wall, was artistically laid out with avenues of acacia trees. Comfortable quarters were built for the staff and visitors ; while the servants had a little village of their own with a mosque and a pond. Their houses were designed in the native style, but were well built and each had its own courtyard.

But though it was all so much improved as regards comfort and appearance, the Chini-Bagh of our early days will always be a happy memory to us.

The Russian Colony had increased enormously, and there were quite a number of ladies and children belonging to different officers connected with the Consulate, Bank, Customs, and some merchants who had settled in Kashgar. One or two of the ladies, who spoke French, I became very friendly with, and liked exceedingly, but mostly the language difficulty and their different mode of life made it impossible for us to be intimate. We simply did not understand each other's ways.

The Russian ladies, when one saw them in the afternoon or evening, were smartly dressed, with very beautiful soft complexions and elaborately dressed hair. But if one happened to call at a house any time during the morning, one found Madame pottering about her household duties in a dressing gown over her night attire, and wearing a boudoir cap. She would not think of dressing until it was time to expect callers for tea. All their social functions began late and did not finish till dawn and after, so the whole household started the day late.

My way of living was just as strange to the Russians, and one day I heard a remark made about " that queer Englishwoman who was in a blouse and skirt with her hair properly done from seven in the morning."

One hardly ever saw a Russian lady wearing a hat. They strolled about in summer (when by chance they did venture out for a so-called walk), elaborately dressed, always carrying a sunshade. In winter a shawl took the place of a hat.

The men mostly wore uniform of some sort, which made them look smart, but rather stiff. Their way of greeting amused me greatly at first. An officer would come up, stop in front of me, click his heels, and salute, then bowing, kiss my hand, salute, clicking his heels again, and the operation was over. It took me a long time to get used to it. I shall never forget the day the regiment arrived, and all the officers, from the Colonel

down, were presented to me in a long stream. Each
officer stood before me, went through his performance,
and passed on for the next man to come. I got so
nervous at last that when a Russian lady standing
near, seeing the funny side of the ceremony, began
to giggle, it was as much as I could do to appear
composed.

The Russians are great people for kissing. The
gentlemen always kiss the ladies' hands and embrace
and kiss each other,—an ordeal my husband often had
to go through, to my great amusement. Our English
visitors dreaded that ceremony when we told them
what they must be prepared for !

When a certain Russian Consul left Kashgar, as my
husband was away, I had to drive out " to the edge
of the carpet," with some of the European community, to see him off. In saying goodbye, he came
to me first, made an elaborate bow, and kissed my
hand, then he took leave of the Russian ladies and, to
my surprise, as he kissed each lady's hand, she stooped
and kissed his bald head. How thankful I was that
my turn had come first, or I should have had to do as
the others did, and oh, that would have been an
ordeal !

Our Russian friends were very gay and sociable,
spending a good deal of time in each other's homes.
Dinner parties were held most evenings at the different
houses, and we were very often among the guests.
Everyone was jovial and friendly, but the dinners
were so slow and so long, and the conversation so
difficult to keep going in a foreign language, or

rather in several foreign languages, that we found the strain of sitting at table from perhaps 9 or 9.30 p.m. till one or two in the morning, very trying. Sometimes between the courses dancing went on to pass the time ; the guests smoked all through the meal, till at last one could hardly see across the room for the haze ; and the atmosphere became stifling. Strong drink likewise was indulged in the whole time, from the vodka, served with the zakuska, or *hors d'œuvres*, to the champagne and liqueurs at the end of the meal, with a dozen sorts of wine between. Being, both of us, non-drinkers, we had a good deal of difficulty often not to give offence by refusing these things which others enjoyed so much. I generally let them fill my array of glasses and left them standing filled. By the time the dinner was halfway through, many of the guests were decidedly lively—and that did not only apply to the men, and before it was over, some had disappeared beneath the table. It was all just a sign of a jolly enter-tainment, and the spirit of good fellowship to the Russians, but, to us, it was rather a trial. One lady actually said to me : " I should not think my husband a man if he did not get drunk ! "

We went through several perfectly horrible meals with the Russians on some of their special festivities. One was on the occasion of a great National fête. The Russians had been celebrating it all day, and when we arrived for the great dinner in the evening, we were received by our host, who dare not leave hold of the door-post to greet us. To my dismay, I saw that the officer I should have on the other side of me at table was in very much the same condition. Of course, we could do nothing, but when we sat down, I was thankful to see that my husband was opposite to me. All through dinner glasses were kept filled, and champagne flowed like water, while my two neighbours became more and more confidential with me, till at last I was almost supporting them as they leant up against me. I did my best to humour them, for they were getting rather quarrelsome, but I was becoming scared and not at all happy ; though I knew my husband was watching, and also several young officers who were sober and disgusted at the affair.

The time came for the Royal Toasts, and our host struggled to his feet and started making a maudlin and unintelligible speech, while he swayed about with his glass of champagne in his hand, the contents of which he gently poured down my shoulder and dress. There was a general rush of gallant young officers with napkins to mop me up, and the speaker subsided in his chair, blissfully unconscious of what had happened. We soon made our escape, and very few of the company even knew that we had gone. But my precious dress was ruined, like most of my other frocks had been in a similar way.

This part of our life and work in Kashgar was both difficult and unpleasant, and the greatest tact was needed at such times to keep our friendly relations from being broken.

As some of the Russians were tennis players, a club was formed. A piece of ground between the two Consulates was rented, and after levelling, two hard courts were made by pounding the ground hard, and then putting on a top-dressing of mud mixed with straw. They could then be kept in condition by water being sprinkled over them every evening. They were not good enough for first rate play, but no one cared about that, for there were no fine players. It gave us exercise and sociability.

Only two of the more enterprising of the Russian ladies actually played, for the others the exertion was too great ; and also they could not bear to be seen in low-heeled shoes and skirts that were wide enough to move freely in. And another difficulty was that one could not play tennis and at the same time hold a sunshade up to protect one's complexion from the sun !

We ladies took it in turns to supply tea twice a week, and we vied with each other as to who could produce the best cakes, ices, or strawberries and cream.

When the regiment came, during the Revolution, the Club became very popular with the young officers, some of whom were keen players.

We were a great source of amusement to the natives. A crowd always gathered along the wall to have an afternoon's entertainment. It was funny enough to see Sahibs running about in hot weather after a ball ; but when the Memsahibs played too, and not always with their own husbands, it was quite past understanding, but very fascinating to watch.

The Swedish colony had grown considerably, and their missionaries had stations in both the Kashgar Cities, Yangi Hissar and Yarkand, where they were did medical work, had schools for children, and held religious services, besides visiting in the homes and making translations of the Bible, hymns, tracts, etc., into Turki. The medical work, especially, flourished, and people flocked to them for treatment.

The Swedes all spoke English, and we always felt that we had very good friends in the Missionaries.

Of course, during all the years we were in Kashgar, we saw many changes in the European Community. My husband outstayed four Russian Consuls ; many of the Swedes, and the Chinese officials were changed. Sometimes it seemed to us as though we were destined to be like the celebrated brook, and go on for ever, regardless of how others came and went.

We always hoped to have three or four visitors a year from the outer world and many noted men stayed with us. They came from all parts of the world to explore, hunt big game, as botanists, naturalists, journalists, and on scientific and archæological missions. The late Dr. Morrison of Pekin paid us a visit, having crossed the whole of China by cart and horseback, in six months. Sir Aurel Stein and Dr. A. von Le Coq both stayed with us several times, when they were on their archæological expeditions.

Dr. Fillipo de Fillipi and his big scientific expedition arrived in 1914 and put up in a house quite near us. I well remember the excitement they caused when they erected a high mast on a little hill behind our garden. This mast was for the aerial of their wireless receiving instrument, by which they hoped they might possibly receive time signals from Lahore. In those days the wireless was little used or understood. With such masses of mountains between us and Lahore, it seemed rather impossible that any wave could come through. We all gathered on this spot at the time specified in the evening, waiting in tense expectation for the signal to come; and great was the excitement when it was clearly heard. We felt that we had been present at one of the greatest discoveries of the century; never dreaming that, in a very few years, we should have wireless receiving sets in every home, on which we could hear music and speech from the other side of the globe, without any high masts or wires, and with an instrument small enough to be contained in a suitcase.

Our Chinese Munshi was standing by while this experiment was being made, and thinking that he was interested, my husband went into a detailed explanation of it all to him. When he had finished his eloquent lecture, the Munshi looked at him very knowingly and said : " Don't expect me to believe that, it is only the Russian Consul down there (pointing to the Russian Consulate) making a noise at the other end of the wire."

Only three English women visited us during all the years I was in Kashgar, though Mr. and Mrs. Littledale had stayed at Chini-Bagh, with my husband, before I went out.

In 1912, my husband heard from India that two ladies, Miss Kemp and Miss MacDougall, wanted to come to Kashgar. We had barely got through the Revolution, and the country was still disturbed, so my husband, not wanting to have any more women to look after, replied very decidedly : " Do not let them come." But being very plucky and afraid of nothing, they came all the same. When we met them, and found what very capable people they were, and that Miss E. G. Kemp was the well-known artist who had done several wonderful journeys in China, we were so glad that they had taken matters into their own hands and had come in spite of an over-cautious Consul-General. They had travelled through Ladak, and over the Karakoram Range, with only native servants, doing a very difficult mountain journey for anyone, and especially for ladies.

Only one who has been cut off from the companionship of her own countrywomen as I had been, can understand what it meant to me to have them staying with us for a time. They arrived in the early autumn, while the weather was still delightfully warm, so, as we were short of rooms owing to the old house being in a state of demolition, and to the building of the new Consulate, we pitched two large comfortable tents for them in the garden under the willows. They said they much preferred them to being in a room, after the open air life they had been living.

Next morning, in the very small hours, Miss Mac-Dougall woke up, to find a disreputable-looking man standing beside her bed, watching her. When he saw she was awake, he made off, and she, not knowing what mischief he meant, ran into Miss Kemp's tent and stayed there. We were very distressed when we heard of her fright, and could not imagine who the man was, or what he was after, though we discovered afterwards that he was a well-known madman. But they certainly could not live out in the garden.

Our Munshi suggested that they should have his guest room, but unfortunately, there was no way to it without going through his wife's quarters, and they would not like that. So we decided to knock a hole in the wall of our stables, which were against the room in question, and put in a temporary door. In Kashgar an alteration of this sort was very easily done. The room was cleaned out, their things moved in, and by afternoon they were established.

At the time, it did not seem at all unusual to put up honoured lady guests in that fashion, and they cheerfully picked their way between our horses by the light of a candle, when they retired to their room that night.

But, looking back on it now, it does seem to me to have been a most primitive way of treating visitors. When one gets into the wilds, one's whole outlook changes, and one adapts oneself to circumstances. Their visit was a very happy time for us all and for me especially.

Our other lady visitor was Miss Ella Sykes, who came with her brother, Brigadier-General Sir Percy Sykes, who officiated for my husband in 1915, when we went home on leave.

The cities of Turkestan had progressed very little. The streets were still as dirty and ill kept, and the people, except for a few rich merchants, lived as they had done for centuries. Many of the Chinese had adopted European dress, which made them look undignified and utterly ridiculous.

When we gave our, or rather my, last New Year's dinner to the Chinese, they came dressed in garments that might have come out of a rag-and-bone shop. The Ti-tai drove from the New City in a closed brougham with a pair of big heavy Chinese ponies. He was wearing a black frock coat, flowered waistcoat, tight black silk trousers evidently made by a Chinese tailor, a bowler hat, and to give the finishing touch to his toilet, his bright green tie was tied round the top of his collar. It was more pathetic than comical to see men who would have been imposing and dignified in their beautiful silks and amber beads making themselves look like scarecrows. One Chinese girl insisted on being married in what she thought was the dress a European girl would wear for such an occasion ; and an enormous flat straw hat loaded with dirty crushed artificial flowers perched on top of her head. Cast-off European clothes were in great demand, especially hats and caps. But one did regret the passing of the beautiful Chinese costumes and ornaments.

A few carriages had appeared on the roads, but very few, for the highways were too badly kept for driving to be indulged in with any degree of comfort. One push bike was ridden by an Andijani boy, and it was at once called by the natives the " Shaitan-Araba " or " Devil's Carriage." Then someone brought a motor cycle, but no one seemed able to find a bad enough name for that. People and horses were terrified of it, and the awful noise it made. I was always afraid of meeting it when we were out riding, and one day suddenly our horses stopped with their ears pricked, and began to tremble, as far away in the distance, we heard the sound of the motor bike. With one leap the horses were up a bank several feet high, and away across the field before we realized what was happening; and the cyclist was obliged to stop to let us get control of them. Ever afterwards they shied at the spot where they had seen the monster. The motor cycle soon disappeared, as the rider found that the roads were too bad and he had to spend all his time cleaning the dust out of the engine.

A very inferior Cinema was started by an Andijani, but I do not think it was a great success, and the films shewn were not calculated to impress the people with a high moral standard of European society.

I shall never forget the marvellous sight we saw in the heavens in 1910. Halley's comet was seen in England, but I fancy it was nothing compared to what we saw in Kashgar. At first it appeared as a morning star and we all got up at three a.m. to see the heavenly body, with its long tail of light. Then for weeks, soon after sunset, the evening sky was lit up by this brilliant star, with a tail stretching halfway across the dome of the sky, broadening out in the shape of a half-closed fan, the brilliancy gradually fading away to the edge, till it was lost in the blue black of the sky. The natives were awestruck at the phenomenon, and tried to find a meaning for it, while the Chinese declared that it had appeared to foretell the death of a great man, or to herald some momentous event to take place in the world. Then the news of King Edward's death came, and the two events were at once connected.

Twice we saw a total eclipse of the sun, when it became quite dark in the middle of the morning, with the stars shining and the birds going to roost. I made a great reputation for myself on the first occasion, for having read of the eclipse in " Whitaker's Almanack," I told the servants in the kitchen that, at ten o'clock next morning, the sun would be put out, and we should all be in darkness. They thought I had gone quite mad, and when ten o'clock came by our time, which was not quite right and they saw us watching the sun, they smiled pityingly at the Memsahib's silliness. Then the light began to fade, and change colour, the dogs started to whine and howl, and presently it was dark as night. Tongues of fire could be seen shooting out round the sun's disc, and all was chilly and uncanny, till the shadow moved off and the world became bright and warm again. I think they credited me with having had something to do with the ordering of the spectacle !

Eclipses of the moon were well known, for the Chinese made such a fuss about them. We sometimes did not know that an eclipse was taking place until we heard the commotion of the beating of drums, kettles, trays, gongs, letting - off of crackers, blowing of trumpets, etc., anything that would make a noise. I even saw our Chinese Munshi sitting outside his door solemnly beating on a tray with a stick. The idea seemed to be that the female element in the world was getting the best of the male element, and must be frightened away. So they made all the noise they possibly could, and took credit to themselves when the shadow moved off the moon.

CHAPTER XIV

GOOD-BYE TO KASHGAR, AND OUR JOURNEY
HOME THROUGH EUROPE IN WAR TIME

At last the time came when the children must go home
to school. Eric was twelve, Sylvia eight, and Robin
three, when my husband applied for furlough early in
1914. Our idea was to leave the family at home, and
for me to return to Kashgar for the last three years
of my husband's service, but we never dreamt of all
that was to happen in that fateful year. Our leave was
granted, and feeling so certain of going, we had an
auction ; packed up our belongings ; and sent off our
heavy boxes ; thinking they would travel more
slowly than we should. We were quite right there,
for they took nearly three years to reach London !

Miss Cresswell's health broke down, and being
anxious to get home, she started, leaving us to wait
for someone to come up to replace my husband.
Then came the news from Pekin that war was declared
between us and Germany, and a telegram from India
saying that all leave was stopped.

Like everyone else, we felt dazed, and did not realize
in the least then what a terrible time was before the
whole world. My own little worries seemed so great
to me. How were we to live with practically no
European stores, and none likely to come ; no winter

clothes, and no possibility of having anything sent; no one to help with the children; and no cook, for the man I had trained had recently died.

I had two big children, who had to be taught, and could not be allowed to run wild; a small boy of three who needed a lot of looking after; and two visitors from India in the house.

My visitors were very thoughtful, and one day when I was really overburdened, one of them, an Officer of the Guides, Captain Blacker, took Eric and gave him a Latin lesson, while the other, Dr. Hayden, the celebrated geologist, made mud pies in the garden with the baby.

However, as usual, we managed somehow, and by dint of hard work the cooking got done, the clothes made, the children looked after, and kept to their lessons, and even a sick Swedish friend nursed for weeks. And so another very happy, busy winter passed, except for the disquieting news from Europe.

We had the Reuter telegrams sent up from Gilgit by each Indian post, and it was quite a business to get the accumulation of a fortnight read through. Although the news was nearly a month late, it was reliable.

Next April my husband got word from India that Brigadier-General Sir Percy Sykes was on his way to Kashgar to relieve him.

So once more we packed up and two days after he arrived with his sister, Miss Ella Sykes, we were off, being in a great hurry to get the mountain part of the journey over before the Terek Pass was closed.

Otherwise we should have to wait for weeks before
the Taldik Pass was open.

The last few days were a nightmare of rush and
work, and to complicate things, Robin contracted a
feverish attack that made us fear that we should have
to put off our going again.

Fortunately he recovered sufficiently for us to make
a start. We wished we could have seen more of the
friends we were leaving behind us at Chini-Bagh, but
we could not wait. I felt so happy that this time there
was to be a lady in charge of the house while I was
away, and I think the servants felt the same.

As I drove out of the courtyard and looked back at
our home, I wondered whether I was leaving it for
good ; and in spite of the prospect of going home to
England, my heart was heavy at the thought.

The mountain roads were in a very bad condition,
due to the thaw ; in many places they were broken
away by the icy water, and the going was both difficult
and dangerous. The worst danger we had to encounter
was from the stones and boulders that, in places, were
rolling and bouncing down the hillsides.

The march to the foot of the Terek Pass was through
a narrow valley, with steep hills on both sides, and we
had to keep to the river bed, picking our way among
the big stones, and it never struck us that those stones
had newly come there. My husband and I were riding
ahead of the party, when suddenly the pony Isa had
been riding, carrying Sylvia in front of him, dashed
past us riderless, setting our horses off at a gallop.
When we had regained control of them and could look

round, there was Sylvia sitting on a boulder crying bitterly and Isa lying some distance away. They were neither of them much hurt, happily, though poor little Sylvia was terrified, and we had difficulty in persuading her to mount a horse again. My husband had a very quiet animal, so he changed mounts with them, thinking that Isa's horse was not trustworthy, and we started off once more. In a very few minutes, the same thing happened, and the same horse, this time ridden by my husband, turned right round and ran back, taking the other horses with him. Then we discovered the cause of it all. Large stones and bits of rock were detaching themselves through the melting of the ice, high up the mountain side, and were bouncing from rock to rock at a tremendous speed. This time the stone passed right in front of us. The pony was one used for carrying the post to Sarikol, and he had learnt by experience what the sound of a crack up the hillside meant, and had saved us by bolting. Over and over again that day he gave us warning, and so we were able to avoid the stones as they came crashing down.

We got up to the rest house at the foot of the pass, Kara Kumush, feeling rather shaken and unnerved; the altitude, too, was making us feel thoroughly depressed and unwell; and we were lying down, trying to get some rest, when Robin, who was playing in the room, caused a diversion by laying his two hands on the red hot pipe of the stove, being attracted to it by the pretty red colour. Of course, he was terribly burnt, and in agony all night. Happily I had with me

ON OUR WAY THROUGH THE THIAN-SHAN RANGE, BETWEEN RUSSIAN
AND CHINESE TURKESTAN.

a rather wonderful remedy for burns, that Dr. von Le Coq had given me when he was in Kashgar, and this I applied at once, and used as a dressing during the whole journey.

Next morning we started up the pass, but found that the road was quite impossible for horses to be ridden on account of the ice and the cut-up condition of the road. Dead and dying ponies, some horribly mutilated and injured, were lying all the way up, with their loads beside them, and vultures were hovering near, waiting till we had passed to begin their dreadful work.

Two Kirghiz said they would carry Sylvia and Robin on their backs in their sleeping sacks, and the children trustfully went with them. Poor little Robin had both hands swathed in bandages, but in spite of it all he was wonderfully brave and cheerful. I was put on a yâk, and started ahead with an old Kirghiz leading the beast, which stumbled and floundered in the melting snow, grunting loudly all the time, and it was all I could do to keep my seat, but, as I do not think I could have walked, I was thankful to be carried up in any fashion. My husband and Eric were obliged to go on foot with the servants. It was a terrible climb and the exertion in the rarefied air put a tremendous strain on the heart. To our dismay, Eric collapsed when he reached the top, and we could do nothing to revive him. Even the brandy that helped the rest of us had little effect on him and we became anxious. He was put up on the yâk behind me, limp as a rag, and almost unconscious, and if I had not kept him leaning against me, by holding his hands firmly round my waist, he would have fallen. It was no easy job to keep us both seated while the yâk went jolting down the pass, the gradient of which was very steep. The other two children on their novel mounts came over quite safely, and the Kirghiz were so careful with them that they earned my deepest gratitude. When we came to the rest house, about one thousand feet down, Eric was suddenly violently sick, and to our surprise and relief recovered completely.

A little further down we came on a horrible sight. Our horses saw it first and began to snort, and show signs of nervousness. Then we saw ahead of us and a little lower down, in a gloomy valley, a caravan of horses and men, the horses still standing but frozen to death, overcome probably by a blizzard. And there too were the vultures at their ghastly work, picking the skeletons clean. We slowly passed them in that veritable valley of death, and left the ghostly caravan behind us. But the memory of it remained with us for many days and nights, and that scene is the most vivid impression of the whole journey left on the children's minds.

Then my courage began to fail me, and the feeling that we should not all survive the journey this time hung over me like a cloud I could not shake off.

Providentially we came safely across the mountains and started off from Andijan once more by train. The heat in Russian Turkestan was very trying after the cold we had experienced in the mountains.

We saw little of the War, beyond crowds of German prisoners all over Russian Turkestan, who did not

look unhappy or badly treated, until we came to
Orenburg, where Cossacks boarded the train, drew
down the blinds, and guarded all the carriage doors
until we had crossed the Volga at Samara.

In Moscow and Petrograd (as it was then called) we
had a very good time, meeting some of our old Kashgar friends. Travelling in Russia at that time was
more pleasant than we had ever known it to be, for
the Tzar's prohibition of alcoholic drink had made
the people so different in manner and behaviour.
Even the mujiks, from being dirty, uncouth-looking
creatures, besotted and half savage with vodka, had
turned into decently behaved people, and all classes
seemed to have improved. Even in the expensive
hotels and restaurants, nothing alcoholic could be
obtained.

The only possible way home from Russia was to
go North, through Finland to Tornea, at the head of
the Gulf of Bothnia, cross the Tornea River, and get
the Swedish train at the terminus of Haparanda, for
Christiania (now Oslo). From Christiania to Bergen,
and then from there to Newcastle.

Almost as soon as we left Petrograd, Cossacks came
on the train, drew all the blinds down in the carriages,
with the order that if any blind was moved, Cossacks on
the line would fire at the offending carriage. We were
passing fortifications at the head of the Gulf of Finland,
and there was a good deal of excitement, for the
Germans were expected to make an advance in that
direction.

We were terrified lest the children, out of curiosity,

should play with the blinds, and were not reassured when we heard that someone had actually been shot through the window for disobeying orders.

After about an hour the blinds were drawn up again, and we stopped to go through a military examination. We had not been warned of this and thinking that we had a long journey before us, we had changed into slippers and had got out books and toys. We were told to take everything out of the carriage and to be quick about it. So we had to bundle out as we were, carrying boots, toys, coats, etc., and a disreputable looking party we made.

Everyone was marched into a big shed, and the examination began. They turned out our pockets, made us hold up our hands while they patted us all over to feel if there were any suspicious swellings that might mean hidden documents. Some people were even being undressed. Later we heard that some ladies had had the heels of their shoes cut off, for someone had been found smuggling messages in her high Cuban heels. My hand bag was turned upside down on the table, and to my embarrassment out came such a collection of things,—hairpins, safety pins, cough lozenges, pencils, bits of rubber, etc.—all the imaginable odds and ends a mother with a family collects on a journey.

In my husband's pocket a very suspicious document was discovered, and our tormentors were triumphant. It was written in Persian, which no one could decipher, and for a moment my husband could not remember how he came to have it. Then he recollected that it was a receipt for some fodder we had bought on the road, which he had stuffed in his pocket and forgotten all about. They made such a fuss that at last my husband told the officer in charge to burn it, and thus make sure it did no harm. He lit a match and burnt it straight away.

Then we were taken one by one into an inner room to be questioned about the amount of money we were taking out of the country. Only a certain sum was allowed to each person. My husband was examined first and came through without any trouble, having shown his private passport with all our names on it. He had an official passport which he was not anxious to use, as he did not wish his official position to be known generally, in case we got into the hands of the Germans when crossing the North Sea. Then my turn came. I was taken up to a table, where an officer was seated with two revolvers before him. Behind me stood three Cossacks with fixed bayonets, the thought of which made my back feel cold and shivery. I was asked what jewellery I had, and how much money. I only showed my Russian money, as I thought that the sixty English gold sovereigns I had sewed in my clothes were no concern of theirs. The Russian money the officer took, and put into a drawer, saying that I was not entitled to take any money out of the country, because my husband had the full amount. I protested that I had as much right as any of the other lady travellers, and besides, as we were travelling with three children, the small amount allowed would not be anything like enough to take us to England. The officer got furious, and asked if I had any gold of any sort. My husband, who was standing by, signalled to me to give him the sovereigns, which I did after a struggle to get them from their hiding place. These he also swept into his drawer and demanded the passport again. So my husband came forward and presented his official passport. At that the officer flew into a perfect rage, asking why he did not say before that he was a British Consul-General, and why he allowed him to take the money. He collected all my roubles and gold from the drawer, and literally throwing them at me across the table, told us to go. Then he turned to another Russian, and grumbled excitedly that he might have got into no end of trouble over those silly English people.

All this time the children had stood patiently hugging their bundles of coats and toys. No one had ever thought of searching them, and they might have had any amount of secret papers and money on them.

So we settled ourselves in the train once more, sincerely hoping we should not have many such experiences. But before reaching the Swedish frontier, we were turned out several times for various examinations.

The train was full of English people, travelling home from China, Persia, and different parts of the East.

The scenery through which we passed was very beautiful. Finland seemed to be composed of woods, lakes, and mountains, and well deserves the name of the " Land of a Thousand Lakes."

We reached Tornea, the terminus of the Finnish Railway, at the very head of the Gulf of Bothnia, in the early morning. It was bitterly cold, and the river was a mass of ice floes. A ferry was waiting to take passengers and their baggage across. We all crowded on deck in the bitter wind, while the ferry, which was also an icebreaker, ground its way slowly through the ice to the other side of the river, where we were told we should have to cross another river,—or a branch of the same Tornea River I suppose it was,—on foot over a bridge. The wind, when we got up on the bridge, was so strong that we could hardly stand against it, and Sylvia and Robin could not get along at all. A kindly Swedish farmer, with a wheelbarrow, seeing our difficulty, picked them up and putting them in his barrow, wheeled them across. Halfway over was the Swedish frontier line, marked by a little toll house, flying the Swedish flag. There we had to pay toll to a jolly old Swede, who, seeing the two children in a wheelbarrow, laughingly declared that they were baggage, and charged accordingly.

The next business was to pass the Swedish medical examination. Typhus was bad in Russia, and the Swedes were doing their utmost to keep it out of their country.

A friendly doctor received us, questioning us as to where we had come from. When he heard we were from Kashgar, he exclaimed : " Do you know my old friend, Dr. Sven Hedin ? " and, finding that we had a mutual friend in him, he took us into his private room, gave us coffee and the dreaded medical examination turned into a very friendly visit. His interesting conversation cheered us up, even as his excellent coffee put warmth into our frozen bodies.

As the train did not leave Haparanda, the terminus of the Swedish railway, till midnight, our doctor friend told us of an hotel near by, where we could spend the day. There we found our fellow passengers collected, and among them a German family. On hearing a disturbance in the passage, we found Eric and two German boys settling the question of the War with fisticuffs. They had to be separated forcibly, while we explained to them that they were in a neutral country and must keep the peace.

Many of the travellers were suffering badly from the cold, for having come from warm climates, they were not prepared with suitable clothing. One family, with small children, had come from Persia, and they had nothing warmer than thin cotton frocks and little knitted coats. It is not surprising that one of these children became seriously ill next day. We happily had the clothes that we had worn in the mountains with us.

About eight o'clock that evening, all the vehicles in the place—farm carts, wagons, carriages of all sorts and sizes, and about two motors—collected outside the hotel, and we passengers, with our baggage, were packed into them. We started out in open vehicles, to drive the twenty odd miles up the Tornea River to Haparanda.

After the War I believe the Swedish and the Finnish railways were joined, and now there is no

difficulty in travelling by this route.   Even when we
did this journey, the Finnish railway ran to a place
immediately opposite Haparanda, but the bridge was
not built, and the river then could only be crossed in
winter by sleigh over the ice.

In spite of the cold, we had a very wonderful drive.
We were not far from the Arctic Circle, and the
scenery and colouring made by the sun that at this
time of the year—in May—barely went below the
horizon at midnight, were different from anything we
had ever seen.

The road ran through pine forests, or along the foot
of wooded hills for the greater part of the way.
Evidently in this Northern region motor cars were
not common, for the sight of one set the cart and
the carriage horses dancing.

From Haparanda we travelled down the length of
Sweden to Orebro, where we branched off to Christiania (Oslo).   From there we had a lovely run to
Bergen.   After crossing a snow-covered pass, we
found ourselves beside the magnificent fiord which
leads right down to the sea at Bergen.

Then came the last and most dreaded bit of the
whole journey—the crossing of the North Sea from
Bergen to Newcastle.   It began to be very rough as
soon as we left the shelter of the land, and as the boat
was carrying no cargo, she pitched and tossed alarmingly.   Most people were too ill to care about anything, my family included.

I spent most of the time watching the man who was
lying along the bows on the look-out for mines.   The

sea was absolutely deserted, and the whole way across we did not see a boat of any description. After I had turned in that night, a friendly English boy knocked at my door with the very superfluous news that we had only just missed running into a mine !

The roughness never abated until we got close up to the coast of Scotland, when the sea calmed down and passengers began to appear. We felt so safe at being close in to our own shores that everyone became cheerful and happy, and we started singing part songs. It was a bit of a shock when we heard on arrival at Newcastle that we had passed over the spot where an hour or two before a large vessel had been sunk off the coast of Aberdeen. The very boat we were on was torpedoed on her return voyage.

After various formalities, we went ashore at Newcastle. The sight of the two real English policemen standing at the gangway made me feel that I must either have a good cry or embrace them, to relieve my feelings. As the latter was out of the question, I had to have recourse to the former as privately as possible.

Next day we were safely home with my mother. She too had been through a time of anxiety, though I purposely did not tell her the exact time we should start on our travels, hoping that she would get our wire from Newcastle, telling of our safe arrival sooner than she expected it.

I had intended returning with my husband after six months, leaving the children at school, but by that time no women were allowed to travel, and he was obliged to go back alone, over the same route, to finish his last three years of service. And so I had taken a final farewell of my home in Central Asia, after a residence there of seventeen years.

INDEX

ABDULLA, death of, 126
Aghachi-Kol, 153
Akbait, 161
Ak-oi, 28, 148, 155
Aksakal, 162
Aksu, 185
Allenbury's Food, 108
Amban, hidden in oven, 188;
smuggled to Russia, 188; wife
and child of, 188, 189
Amu-Daria, 7
Anderson, Mr., 153
Andijan, 2, 8, 11; drive to, 105;
met by Kashgar servants at, 13;
stay at, 12.
Anna Bibi, shrine of, 131
Aral Sea, 51, 157
Aris, 152, 180, 181
At-Bashi, 162; River, 162; crossing
river of, 163; stay at, 164
Aulie-Ata, 175
Aylesbury Dairy Company, 108

BABIES, 127; baby found, 128
Baker, Amban hidden by, 188
Baku, 5
Bargai, 150
Bargain, making of, 72
Beggar, mad, 132
Beli-voda, 177
Bergen, 223, 229
Bhang, 60
Birds, of Kashgar, 119
Blacker, Captain, 218
Bostan Terek, 136, 142, 143
Bower, Captain, 56
British Consul, 62; Consul-General,
62
British Consulate, 109
British Consulate-General, 35; build-
ing of, 201, 202
British Foreign Office, 203

Buchanan, Sir George, 200
Buddha, stucco figurines of, 55
Bukhara, 7
Burman defile, 172
Buran, 116; Amban's life saved by,
192

CALF, stuffed, 92, 93
Caravan, frozen, 222
Caspian Sea, 2, 4, 5
Chadir Kul Lake, 157
Chakmak, 154
Charms, 127
Cheras, 60
Children, 123, 124, 126, 127
Chimkent, 178, 179, 180
Chinaman's gallantry, 74
Chinese, boy wounded, 189; carts,
137; dinner, 76; dress, change
of, 213; Empire, 58; ladies, visit
of, 44; Legation in London, 61;
Munshi, 45, 210; New City, 63;
shops, 79; soldiers, 79; Turke-
stan, 51, 52, 53, 56, 59, 61
Chini Bagh, 30, 203, 219
Christiania, 223
Chu River, 172
City gate, blowing open of, 195
Climate of Kashgar, 113, 114, 115
Coats' cotton, 74
Cow, milked by small boy, 93;
worshipped by Hindu, 93, 94
Cramer, piano made by, 17, 47
Cresswell, Miss Annie, 190, 193
201, 217

DINNER party, Hindu, 97; Mohammedan, 97; to Chinese Ambans,
97; to Russians, 100
Divorce, 129
Dolan Pass, 169

233

Donald, 185, 191, 192
Dust storm, 115

Eagles, 117
Eclipse, of sun, 215 ; of moon, 215
Elliman's Embrocation, 168
Eric, 107, 108, 137, 152, 163, 175,
    176, 178, 180, 181, 182, 192, 217,
    221, 222

FILLIPI, Dr. Fillipo di, 209
Finland, 223 ; examination at fron-
    tier of, 224
Fleas, 139

GARDENER gathering mulberries,
    120
German prisoners, 222
Gilgit, 112
Glass in Kashgar, 35
Godwin Austin peak, 55

HALLEY'S Comet, 214, 215
Han dynasty, 58
Haparanda, 223, 229
Hashish, 60
Hat, my winter, 110
Hayden, Dr., 218
Heath, Miss Fannie, 108
Hedin, Dr. Sven, 116, 227
Hendricks, Father, 36, 48, 49
Hoernle, Professor, 56
Högberg, Elsa, 47
Högberg, Mr., 30, 37, 47, 88, 136,
    143, 187, 201
Högberg, Mrs., 31, 47, 136, 143
Hsien-Kuan, 63, 186 ; wife and
    son of, 187
Hsie-tai, 41, 42, 43, 63, 99, 189, 199
Hunter, Mr., 185, 186, 191
Hunza, 112

ID-GA Mosque, 65
Ikon, 169, 180
Irkeshtam, 26, 27, 104

Isa Akhun, 88, 89, 93, 105, 153, 163,
    166, 219, 220
Issykul Lake, 170

JAFAR ALI, 18, 20, 42, 84, 105, 109
Jafar Bai, 137
Jagatai Turki, 59
Jigda, 119
John, 153, 168, 173, 180, 181

K2, 55
Kang, 81
Kan-su, 51
Kara-Balti, 173
Kara-Ghulak, 162
Karakoram Mountains, 52, 211
Kara-kumush, 220
Kara-su, 160
Karateki Pass, 153
Kara-unkur, 167
Kazi-Kalan, 139, 140
Kazan, 163
Kek-lik, 67, 144
Kemp, Miss E. G., 210, 211, 212
Khotan, 54 ; carpets, 60
Kidnapping, of girl, 130
Kirghiz, 18, 21, 22, 23, 141, 142,
    143, 144, 145 ; dinner to, 149 ;
    encampments, 27, 28, 29 ; felts,
    60 ; feeding bottle, 147, 148 ;
    houses, 147 ; women, 146
Kissing, Russian custom of, 205
Kizil-su, 25, 33
Kolokoloff, Mme., 48
Kongur Peak, 34
Kornilovski, 176
Krasnovodsk, 4, 5, 6
Kublai-Khan, 73
Kulbastai, 176
Kumbelata, 170
Kumiss, 145, 162
Kun-lun Mountains, 52
Kutemaldi, 170

LADAKH, 53
Ladies, Chinese, visit of, 43 ; visit
    to, 81

Lassoo, 101
Le Coq, Professor A. von, 56, 183,
    209, 221
Littledale, Mr. and Mrs., 210
Lop Nor, 25, 52, 157

MacDougall, Miss M., 210, 211,
    212
Manuscripts, ancient, 55, 56
Maralbashi, 25 ; road, 198
Marco Polo, 73
Mare's milk, 145
Margillan, 8
Marmots, 157
Marpa, 77
Medinsky, General, 8, 10
Mediterranean, 5
Men's dress, 69, 70
Merchants, Chinese, 79
Miles, Captain P. J., 103, 109
Mingyol, 29
Minkeldi, Mons. and Mme., 181, 182
Morrison, Dr., 209
Moscow, 223
Mother, my, 1, 103, 110, 230
Motor-bicycle, 213, 214
Mujik, sick woman, 168
Mullah, 138
Musicians, women, 122, 123

Nan-shan Mountains, 52
Naryn, 152, 165, 166
Nasha, 60
Nestorian Christians, 57
Newcastle, 223, 229
Nicholson, Sir Arthur, 61, 62
Nurse, 177, 178

Old Kashgar city, 63
On-Archa, 167
Orebro, 229
Orenburg, 223
Osh, 2, 13, 17
Ovis poli, 144
Oxus, 7, 51

Pamirs, 8, 34, 51, 53
Parcels, from home, 110
Persian Mountains, 6

Petrograd, 223
Petrovsk, 4, 5
Petrovsky, Mons., 29, 35, 48, 56
Piano, 17, 46, 47
Pishpek, 172
Plum pudding, 100
Post, to Kashgar, 112
Powell, Colonel, 90, 91
Prohibition of drink in Russia, 223

Raquette, Dr., 47, 48
Raquette, Mrs., 40, 47
Robin, 101, 201, 217, 219, 220, 221
    227
Rostov, 3
Russo-Asiatic Bank, 64
Russian, Bear, 60 ; Consulate, 61
    dinner party, 206 ; Foreign Office
    200 ; Government, 60, 61 ; stoves,
    35, 114 ; Turkestan, 104, 157.

Samara, 223
Samarkand, 8, 11
Samovar, 3, 15
Sarikol, 112
Sea-slugs, 83, 85
Semiretchia, province of, 152
Shrines, 131
Shuttleworth, Captain, 152
Smallpox, 124, 125
Smugglers, 26
Singer sewing machines, 74
Sokoff, Mons., 185, 193
Soldiers, 79
Soup, swallow's nest, 83
Speke, Mr. John, 11, 12
Spring, in Kashgar, 118
Srinagar, 112
Stein, Sir Aurel, 56, 57, 209 ; collec-
    tion at British Museum, 58
Sturgeon, 6
Sukalak, 172
Summer, evenings, 120
Sunni Mohammedans, 58
Swedish colony, 202, 208 ; farmer,
    227 ; medical examination, 227 ;
    mission station, 64; nurses, 189,
    190.

Sykes, Sir Percy, 212, 218
Sykes, Miss Ella, 212, 218
Sylvia, 110, 137, 152, 177, 178, 180,
    181, 217, 219, 220, 221, 227

TAGHARMA Peak, 55
Taklamakan Desert, 56
Taldik Pass, 219
Tamerlane, tomb of, 9
Tao-tai, 42, 61, 63, 184 ; and wife,
    murder of, 186, 189
Tarantass, 2, 14
Tartars, 163
Tashkent-Moscow Railway, 182
Tengri Nor, 55
Tennis club, 207
Terek Pass, 22, 218, 221, 222
Thian-Shan Mountains, 2, 16, 34, 53,
    55, 104, 155
Thief, 111
Tibet, 51
Tion-debba, 156
Ti-tai, 76, 77, 85, 190, 193, 195, 197,
    213 ; wife of, 81, 84, 85.
Tokmak, 172
Tornea, 223, 227 ; River, 227
Trans-Caspian Railway, 2
Trees, of Kashgar, 119
Tunganis, 166
Tung-shang, 63
Turfan, 55
Turgat Pass, 156, 157
Tzagan, Mons., 26, 27
Tzar's groom, 4

ULUGHCHAT, 27
Union Jacks, 186, 193
Urumtchi, 197

VOLGA, 223
Vyernyi, 170

WALK in city, 74, 75
Washer-woman, 127
Water of Kashgar, 96
Welcome to Russian troops, 194, 195
Whitaker's Almanac, 215
Wireless signals, 210
Witch doctor, 125
Woman, rescue of, 133
Women of Kashgar, 121 ; dancing
    of, 123 ; dress of, 70, 71

YAMÊN, 81, 184 ; Ti-tai's, 77, 80
Yamstchik, 14, 170
Yâk, 17, 18
Yang-Ta-jen, 41, 43, 189
Yangi-Hissar, 191
Yarkand, 54, 60
Yellow River, 52
Younghusband, Captain, 35, 60, 61
Yuen Taotai, 184

ZAITSEFF, Colonel and Mme., 16, 17

Some other Oxford Paperbacks for readers
interested in Central Asia, China and
South-east Asia, past and present

CAMBODIA

GEORGES COEDES
ANGKOR: AN INTRODUCTION

CHINA

HAROLD ACTON
PEONIES AND PONIES

PETER FLEMING
THE SIEGE AT PEKING

W. SOMERSET MAUGHAM
ON A CHINESE SCREEN

G.E. MORRISON
AN AUSTRALIAN IN CHINA

OSBERT SITWELL
ESCAPE WITH ME! AN ORIENTAL
  SKETCH-BOOK

ALBERT VON LE COQ
BURIED TREASURES OF CHINESE
  TURKESTAN

AITCHEN WU
TURKISTAN TUMULT

INDONESIA

S. TAKDIR ALISJAHBANA
INDONESIA: SOCIAL AND
  CULTURAL REVOLUTION

VICKI BAUM
A TALE FROM BALI

MIGUEL COVARRUBIAS
ISLAND OF BALI

JACQUES DUMARCAY
BOROBUDUR

JENNIFER LINDSAY
JAVANESE GAMELAN

EDWIN M. LOEB
SUMATRA: ITS HISTORY AND
  PEOPLE

MOCHTAR LUBIS
TWILIGHT IN DJAKARTA

MADELON H. LULOFS
COOLIE

ANNA MATHEWS
THE NIGHT OF PURNAMA

COLIN McPHEE
HOUSE IN BALI

HICKMAN POWELL
THE LAST PARADISE

BERYL DE ZOETE AND
  WALTER SPIES
DANCE AND DRAMA IN BALI

E.R. SCIDMORE
JAVA, GARDEN OF THE EAST

LADISLAO SZEKELY
TROPIC FEVER: THE ADVENTURES
  OF A PLANTER IN SUMATRA

EDWARD C. VAN NESS AND
  SHITA PRAWIROHARDJO
JAVANESE WAYANG KULIT

MALAYSIA

ABDULLAH ABDUL KADIR
THE HIKAYAT ABDULLAH

ISABELLA BIRD
THE GOLDEN CHERSONESE

PIERRE BOULLE
SACRILEGE IN MALAYA

C.C. BROWN (Editor)
SEJARAH MELAYU OR MALAY ANNALS
JOHN M. CHIN
THE SARAWAK CHINESE
COLIN N. CRISSWELL
RAJAH CHARLES BROOKE: MONARCH OF ALL HE SURVEYED
HENRI FAUCONNIER
THE SOUL OF MALAYA
JOHN D. GIMLETTE AND H.W. THOMSON
A DICTIONARY OF MALAYAN MEDICINE
A.G. GLENISTER
THE BIRDS OF THE MALAY PENINSULA, SINGAPORE AND PENANG
TOM HARRISSON
WORLD WITHIN
DENNIS HOLMAN
NOONE OF THE ULU
SYBIL KATHIGASU
NO DRAM OF MERCY
R.J. WILKINSON (Editor)
PAPERS ON MALAY SUBJECTS
RICHARD WINSTEDT
THE MALAY MAGICIAN

PHILIPPINES
AUSTIN COATES
RIZAL

SINGAPORE
R. ST. J. BRADDELL
THE LIGHTS OF SINGAPORE
PATRICK ANDERSON
SNAKE WINE: A SINGAPORE EPISODE
C.E. WURTZBURG
RAFFLES OF THE EASTERN SEAS

THAILAND
MALCOLM SMITH
A PHYSICIAN AT THE COURT OF SIAM
ERNEST YOUNG
THE KINGDOM OF THE YELLOW ROBE

TIBET
PETER FLEMING
BAYONETS TO LHASA